The Wallstrip™ edge

Using Trends to Make Money— Find Them, Ride Them, and Get Off

HOWARD LINDZON

BUSINESS PLUS

NEW YORK   BOSTON

Charts courtesy of bigcharts.com and Eric Crittenden of Blackstar Funds.

Business Plus
Hachette Book Group
237 Park Avenue
New York, NY 10017
Visit our Web site at www.HachetteBookGroup.com.

Business Plus is an imprint of Grand Central Publishing.
The Business Plus name and logo are trademarks of Hachette Book Group, Inc.

Printed in the United States of America

First Edition: February 2009

10 9 8 7 6 5 4 3 2 1

Library of Congress Cataloging-in-Publication Data
Lindzon, Howard.
    The wallstrip edge : using trends to make money—find them, ride them, and get off / Howard Lindzon.—1st ed.
        p. cm.
    Includes index.
    ISBN: 978-0-446-50864-3
    1. Stocks. 2. Portfolio management. 3. Investment analysis. 4. Investments. I. Title.
    HG4661.L557 2009
    332.6—dc22

                                                                    2008019571

CONTENTS

INTRODUCTION

To the Optimists Go the Spoils

We live in a media-filled world of Doom and Gloomers. Too bad for them. They miss all the opportunities and, despite what anyone tells you, making money in the stock market is possible, can be fun, mostly honest—and you're goddamn right.

The world has "shrunk" and true global markets are at your fingertips. Markets can all move together for periods of time, but for the most part you should look at the investing world as a market of STOCKS. This market of stocks is full of "Beauties" as well as "Beasts." We are surrounded by trends; we live in a free country and do not understand the basic mechanics of the stock market. Here is a quick lesson: It is all about supply and demand and mood.

We live in a capitalist society but we don't teach investing in grade school. We should. Kids would invest better than us. They have less greed, fear, and anxiety. Most important, they are optimistic.

The years 2003 through 2007 were sweet ones for trend followers in the stock market. The emergence of China, India, Russia, Mexico, and Brazil; ETFs, low interest rates, and a weak U.S. dollar all created a perfect storm for equities around the globe. That was changing fast in late 2007, early 2008.

Winners were everywhere. Homebuilders, Internet stocks, oil, gold, emerging markets, iPods, iMacs, BlackBerries, rubber shoes, condoms, exotic dancers, guns, ammunition, aerospace, agriculture, solar power, water...the list goes on and on. By the time you read this book, many if not all of these trends will be long gone or on the way out. No matter, new trends will emerge. They always do. What you need is a simple way to track the new leaders so that when they emerge, you are ready to ride them. You will find those tools and directions in this book.

If you are reading this book, you will probably be interrupted 500 times by phone calls, e-mails, pings, pokes, text messages, kids, sleep, your blog, reading other blogs, your dog, and Twitter. If you are so engrossed as to read this wonderful book in one sitting, you will have all the above waiting for you once you are done. (And by the way, your family will be pissed.) We live in a world with distractions. On the optimistic side, those who manage them best will be rewarded with wealth.

When you watch an NFL football game today, notice how the offense and defense are built around distraction and misdirection. It's a game within the game. The stock market is no different. Technology has allowed noise into our lives for good and bad, but the basics of investing have not changed. Bankers, brokers, analysts, talking heads, tipsters, and the rest of old and new media are in the business of making noise. The key is to control that information in 2008 and beyond.

For all the noise and distraction, the idea is to have your investment dollars appreciate as much as possible. Consider Warren Buffett. He has not changed his style in fifty years. He has used technology to build risk management vehicles, but basically he buys low in hopes of selling higher (at least he thinks so). In the stock market, you buy great companies and you are generally rewarded over time; you buy them at the right time and price and you do even better. You learn how to sell them properly and you have mastered the trade. If you learn to cut your losers fast, before they become big losers, you may not get wealthy but you won't lose your fortune. Pretty easy...

I wish!

The stock market is difficult; investing is not easy. Investing with discipline may be one of the hardest things we can do well. But it is not nearly as hard as the "experts" would lead you to believe. This book is not a get-rich-quick diatribe. There is no "green light/ red light" system for buying and selling your way to stock market riches. Those books have been written. If you are not open to the idea that you can make money without the advice you get from your TV, then this book is not for you. If you are going to follow trends, TV is the worst investment of your time.

I do believe that if you are going to invest you should do so with the goal of not just matching the universally accepted averages that mutual funds compete against (the Dow, Standard and Poors, Wilshire 5000), but with the intention of trouncing them.

We all want to own the next Starbucks. (In fact, a book with that title has been written. Catchy.) Trust me, I will help you do that. I will also teach you that you don't need the next Starbucks. Damn, as I write this book, Starbucks sits more than 65 percent below its all-time high of $40 in January 2008. (Maybe Starbucks is the next Starbucks.) You can find hundreds of great wealth-building companies short of the next Starbucks that will create great wealth for you. If I helped you do just that, this would be a short book. Therefore, I will help you find the next Starbucks—many of them—ride them, and, most important, teach you how to get off.

The media and textbooks are busy preaching how you should buy low, sell high. It makes perfect sense. Most businesses are based around that principle; otherwise they would not make profits and be able to pay bills. Here is what I always say in return: Great stocks hit all-time highs. They hit them over and over. This book is not a holy grail. Money management is the holy grail. Money management is very personal, and I will spend a lot of this book—and Chapter 5 specifically—on the subject.

Your next question may be: What makes me qualified to write a book on trends? If I am so smart, why should I take the time to share my thoughts and write a book? Great questions, and ones you should ask of every book and financial author. First off, I love to write. It's a curse/blessing. It helps me think about ideas, flesh them out, get feedback, and look at them in a new light.

This book is for those who want to be more actively involved in their financial future and learn about the pitfalls that I have faced in over ten years of actively managing a hedge fund and investing in all aspects of the stock market and private markets. It is not just about winners. I have made mistakes on the path to my success today as a husband, father, partner, investor, and friend, and I'll talk about them.

When you finish the book, I believe you will have all the basic tools to invest in long-term winners in the stock market. Throughout the book I will emphasize the following:

- Turn off your TV. That won't help you beat the pros.
- You should cancel your financial periodicals. They are just contributors to the noise and your anxiety.
- You should trade less and cut your costs.
- You should use a discount brokerage.
- You should hunt for the next big winners from the all-time high list, not the all-time low list.
- You can learn to spot the disruptive leaders. It will take the most work, but I will give you eleven years worth of shortcuts from my experiences and the fastest ways to find information. I have never kept them secret, but I am using the book to organize my history of thoughts on investing to date.
- You *must* learn how to sell. I guarantee I will show you what to buy and when to buy it. You must take responsibility for selling to manage your profits and losses.
- You *must* have a better attitude to invest. Short sellers are nowhere near the Forbes 500 list. Entrepreneurs and "can do" people with positive attitudes get there.

CHAPTER 1

Turn Off Your TV

Don't trust Whitey.

THE JERK

Noise is an investor's worst enemy. It leads to fear, anxiety, and countless investing mistakes. But we as investors are constantly inundated with headlines. They proclaim bad news because it sells. It also generates commissions. If you turn off the TV, control the flow of information, and stand farther back, your stock market returns will improve.

That seems very hard for most Americans because we're fascinated with the stock market. We all want to find the next Google (note: Google may still be the next Google), Dell, or Microsoft. CNBC knows you, and that's how it profits. But I say, turn the TV off. I will show you a better way, a quieter way, a more peaceful way, and, ultimately, a more profitable way to invest in the stock market.

You watch an NFL football game nowadays and both the offense and defense are built around distraction and misdirection. Technology has allowed noise into our lives for good and bad. The technology creep has mostly been great. Investing, though, has never changed. Bankers, brokers, analysts, "talking heads," tipsters, and the rest of old and new media are in the business of noise making. The good news is that you are the one in control of that information in 2009 and beyond. For all the noise and distraction, the idea is to have your investment dollars appreciate as much as possible. Consider Warren Buffett. He has not changed his style in fifty years. He has used technology to build risk-management vehicles, but basically he buys low in hopes of selling higher. In the stock market, you buy great companies and you are generally rewarded over time. You buy them at the right time and price and you do even better. You learn how to sell them properly and how to cut your losses, and you have mastered the game.

To the Optimists Go the Spoils

The years 2003 through 2007 were sweet ones for stock market trend followers. The emergence of China, India, Russia, Mexico, and Brazil, exchange traded funds (ETFs), low interest rates, and a weak U.S. dollar policy created a perfect storm for equities.

Homebuilders, Internet stocks, oil, gold, emerging markets, iPods, iMacs, BlackBerries, rubber shoes (Crocs), condoms, exotic dancers, guns, ammunition, aerospace, agriculture, solar—the list goes on and on. By the time you read this book, many, if not all, those trends will be long gone or on their way out. In late 2007 and early 2008, many of these trends did indeed end.

No matter—new trends will emerge. They always do. What you need is a simple way to track the new leaders so that when they emerge you are ready to ride them. You will find those tools and directions in this book.

Opportunity Knocks—Every Day!

The stock market offers opportunity for every economic condition, every single day. That's one of its greatest gifts to investors. We miss the opportunities because we are often paralyzed by our investment mistakes. The stock market is difficult. It isolates your weakness, exposes it, and, if you are not careful, inflicts great financial damage.

With over 12,000 actively traded stocks in the U.S. market and exchange traded funds (ETFs) exploding, opportunity should always be your focus. You may never find the "perfect" investment, but I will be beating into your heads how to prune and cut your losers. If you are not holding losers, those in distribution mode by Wall Street, you will be free to focus on opportunities. In other words, you will be way ahead of the game.

The goal throughout your investment life should be to catch winners, focus on those winners, and cut your losses. The great news is that opportunities are plentiful and are leaving the starting blocks to big returns daily. There is no advice on how to get rich quick in this book, but there is a long discussion with examples of how you can find, ride, and get off great stock trends. There is work involved to get there. Throughout this book I will constantly write about staying in the game. Once you begin to invest, the temptations and thrills can become intoxicating. It is human nature. The taste of freedom and money has created this thrill since the beginning of time.

When in Doubt Watch *Seinfeld*

In a classic *Seinfeld* episode, George Costanza tells Jerry and Elaine, "Every decision I have ever made in my entire life has been wrong. Every instinct I have in every aspect of life—it's all been wrong." After a discussion about whether chicken salad or salmon salad is the true opposite of tuna salad, Jerry advises George to do the opposite of what his instinct is telling him. Jerry says, "If every instinct you have is wrong, then the opposite would have to be right."

George concludes, "I will do the opposite." The result is a date with a beautiful woman and a job with the New York Yankees.

The Blame Game Is for Losers

We love to blame. When doing yoga, I blame my parents for bad genetics. When I get burned on a stock, I blame the company's CEO (I know that won't help). Turn on the television and you will see CNN blame the Republicans and Fox blame the Democrats. Controversy adds to the noise, but it sells. Short-sellers blame Alan Greenspan for the market going up and now those who bought homes on easy credit blame Alan Greenspan for tricking them. But it doesn't pay to blame stocks or the stock market. If you want to be a successful investor, take responsibility for your money and decisions.

Opinions Are Like Assholes: Everybody Has One

You ask for an opinion and you will get one. Actually, you will get opinions whether or not you ask for them. So just stop asking.

Price Targets Should Be Banned!

I don't trust people who issue price targets for stocks, which means I have developed a deep disdain for Wall Street research. The price of each stock you own will do the work for you, based on your own money-management strategy. Upward-trending growth stocks are hard to value. Therefore, the analysts on Wall Street issuing price targets are just guessing as well. They're a tool for analysts in order for them to feel relevant. In the end, price targets are just noise that will get in the way of you *holding* your winners.

If You Want to Invest, Be Prepared to Suck at Times!

We all have our own journey and stock market stories. Like many Americans I have always been fascinated by the stock market. I was just a teenager when I made my first stock purchase, a Canadian beverage company called Clearly Canadian. I was "clearly" wrong. It was a hot stock, and a stockbroker I was golfing with urged me to buy it. I did. I believe it was in the twenties. I believe I sold it at three. Buying high and selling low was not intoxicating. I was trend following—in reverse. I quickly gave up on the stock market. Betting football and drinking was a better intoxication.

My very first job was in the fall of 1987 as an order-entry clerk at a small brokerage house in Toronto. That's right—right before the crash of 1987. Talk about timing. I was now two for two. I vividly recall Black Monday. I had no money, so it's not that I lost any, but I remember the crazy flow of orders that day. I worked in the cage, which was off limits to brokers. Brokers put their order slips—green for buy and pink for sell—on a machine that swept the orders to our terminals for us to enter.

On that Monday the pink slips were flying in. Brokers were pounding on our locked door. It was total chaos. I remember having to input them that night and having to miss the Maple Leafs hockey game—I was pissed. Needless to say, I was let go by November and headed back to graduate school.

My first *real* job after graduate school was as a stockbroker, and I still knew absolutely nothing. Now I was three for three. And in spite of my horrific stock market experiences, I found myself once again coming back to the stock market. It must have been fate. In any event, I was a Canadian citizen looking for sponsorship so I could stay in the U.S. I answered an advertisement in the newspaper (how quaint). I got the job.

Looking back, I would have been more successful as a stockbroker if I had left it at that and just sold what they gave me. Instead of selling stocks to unsuspecting cold calls, I wanted to take everything in, try every investing style, and own every stock.

The first stock I ever truly got behind was Bank of Boston. The year was 1991 and the stock was basically a penny stock. Despite my dual master's degree in finance, I knew squat about the real world. No wonder one of my favorite movies is *Back to School* starring Rodney Dangerfield. The U.S. was in a real recession, the RTC was in full force, and bank stocks were poison. In short, it was definitely not a stock in an uptrend. That said, Bank of Boston was a home run. I was lucky—and totally hooked.

Flash forward a few years and careers. I remember the first time I read an article from Jim Cramer. It was back in 1997, and I used to read *Smart Money*. Jim was writing about the bull market in Intel and semiconductors. He was dead-on at the time. The market had been good for years. I was a young, eager entrepreneur and loved the stock market. The bull market in the NASDAQ and small capitalization stocks made me look smart. I liked reading everything—Jim's editorials the most.

When Jim started TheStreet.com, my hedge fund was up and running. It was the summer of 1998. We were a start-up, didn't have much money to manage—mostly friends and family—but we cared deeply. So did Cramer. I was an early subscriber and loyal. It was not so much that I was getting ideas from Jim and the Web site, but I was truly inspired by the overall passion of his writing. It was his entrepreneurial spirit toward the new medium: the Internet and its impact on the financial world.

As my friend Fred Wilson, an Internet venture capitalist and investor in TheStreet.com and Wallstrip, once said to me: "Cramer was the original blogger." He was so intense. Jim would bang out twenty posts a day from his "trading desk" on Wall Street. It was a play-by-play, the ESPN of stocks. The early days of the financial Web were shaped by Jim Cramer and TheStreet.com, and to the early pioneers went the spoils. Jim Cramer and TheStreet.com got their share.

Today, Jim is a television celebrity. His sixty-minute daily CNBC show, combined with his prolific writing and CNBC hosting appearances, are now impossible to track. Unfortunately, I think his message has been lost in the noise. The sheer number of his articles, posts, and ideas has made it impossible to keep up. There are many Web sites dedicated to just the tracking of

Jim's picks and pans. Go figure. Watching TheStreet.com succeed against what seemed like an impossible business niche against the *New York Times*, the *Wall Street Journal*, and the hundreds of business magazines was inspiring.

But, as much as I admire Jim Cramer for all he has done for pioneering financial media, CNBC and financial television have now taken it away. I don't believe it serves a purpose for the audience that watches it the most. There's just too much noise being thrown at us on a daily basis. To me, the average investor is now best served by doing less and cutting costs to the bone. Learn to control the noise so you can find trends.

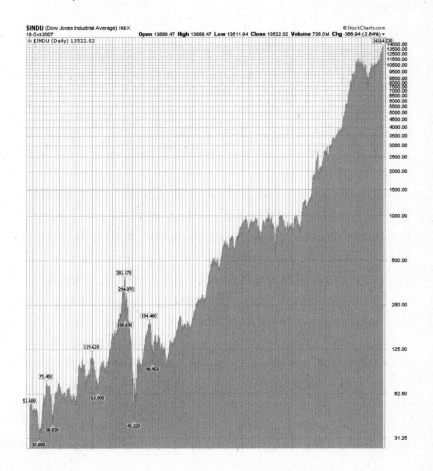

Trounce the Averages

I believe everyone should own individual stocks. Take a look at the very long-term pricing chart of the Dow Industrials:

If you are comfortable matching the indexes, which are not bad returns, you should index. If you are going to own stocks, remember that the returns won't be linear. Some years will be fantastic and others downright miserable. But if you are going to invest in stocks, and plan to finish this book, you should do so with a goal to trounce the averages. Keep this in mind, though: Goldman, Merrill, Morgan Stanley, and the rest of the investment banks might be important for Corporate America, but are probably not so good for the individual investor.

Invest or Trade

Here is a rule I try to live by: *Never let trades turn into investments, but be willing to let investments become trades.* Everything I own is for sale at the right price. If I am trading (very rare), I have learned to be very focused on the boundaries I set for the trade. When I get lazy, I lose money.

We all exchange our services for money. Doctors with patients, lawyers with clients, and on and on. I get asked all too frequently how to make more money from trading the stock market. I tell people to build their business with their extra time, learn to knit, cat juggle, or take their family to the beach. Investing money in the stock market requires a commitment to excellence and longer-term thinking.

Ask yourself the same question as well: Why not get more customers, learn to market your business, and invest in yourself? You will get much better returns for your efforts than you will trading stocks.

I hear too many people refer to their stock accounts as "gambling money." Your gambling money should be for Vegas, where there is not a positive expectancy. Unlike Vegas, you can actually make money in the stock market, so never compare the two.

Shut Off CNBC!

Back to CNBC. You should really consider turning off CNBC for these three reasons: It has little financial value, it creates anxiety, and it is a one-way communicator. You need to get very quiet to hear what is most important and meaningful.

I understand that television is part of our culture and has persisted and thrived particularly in the financial sector. TV is everywhere. But just because it is always on doesn't mean it is important—and just because someone is talking to you on the tube doesn't mean they have something valuable to say.

Let me put this another way. The major events of our time that you just can't miss and that you won't forget mark individual time frames during which trends in the market begin, end, accelerate, or decelerate. For example, the stock market had been going down hard for two years before September 11.

The tragedy marked the beginning and end of many trends while accelerating and decelerating many others. But serious trend following is not about, How might I make money on the day after 9/11? Consider travel-related companies and stocks: Heading into 9/11, they were very weak. For weeks after, they were decimated. The terrorist attacks of 9/11 accelerated the market bloodshed. But it was only six months to a year later that the market bounced back and they passed their pre-9/11 prices and accelerated to the upside.

This defied all logic—at least in the eyes of the financial media. Hilton Hotels, which they couldn't give away just after 9/11, was sold in 2007 in one of the largest private equity deals of all time. As it turned out, hotel stocks were among the best investments post-9/11, and you didn't have to be an expert to understand that the movement of the stock's price was signaling something important.

In hindsight, price dictated the strong trend. The hotel strength came from many factors, the biggest being a curious world and a weak U.S. dollar. Most humorous to me is how the "rich and smart" bankers are, it seems, really closet trend-followers. They have all the tools and capital to do fundamental analysis, so was Hilton not a better buy in 2002?

In the last few years, there have been only a few major news events that have really mattered to the financial markets, events that have risen above the noise of the daily news. The South Asian tsunami, September 11, Hurricane Katrina, the Chinese economic boom, the outsourcing of jobs to India, and the United States' war in Iraq and "credit crunch" all come to mind. Big money has been made off these trends. But to see them for the investment opportunities they truly present, you can't be bogged down in the daily headlines. While Britney tries to clean herself up, while Paris Hilton did time (Martha Stewart too) and aspiring politicians sound-bite each other to death, trend followers—not headline watchers—have made gigantic money. For example, the closed-end Malaysian (EWM) fund has been on a tear since the tsunami, China's boom has led to a major trend run in commodities, India's workforce has increased productivity and leverage for thousands of American and foreign companies big and small, and the war in Iraq has meant a boom for aerospace and defense stocks.

A premise of trend following is that money flows and continues to flow for long periods of time before it ends, until reason is finally out the window. In my opinion and from my experience, the market is irrational 99 percent of the time on its way to rationality. It gets there when it finally decides to get there, and that happens very quickly. If you do not manage the noise, you risk being scared into doing something stupid, so the less noise the better. Don't let the so-called TV experts confuse you.

Why Most Active Money Managers Can't Beat the S&P

The payoff structure for common stocks is highly skewed to a small minority. Take a look at the chart below, which graphs the distribution of stock winners:

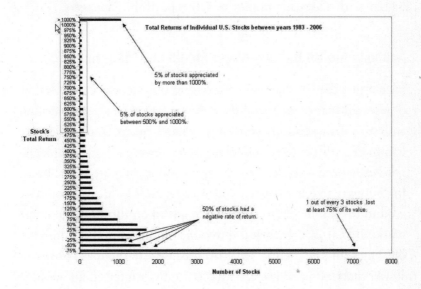

The chart is really quite amazing, but not that surprising if you have ever started a company. For every Microsoft there are hundreds of software companies that go bankrupt, or at best are dead money. There were fifty-plus car manufacturers in the United States in the 1950s. Ford, GM, and Chrysler were the only survivors for decades. Seventy-four percent of all stocks actually underperform the S&P during their lifetime. My friend Eric Crittenden at Blackstar has done the back testing to see that the only way to outperform the S&P consistently is to disproportionately own the other 26 percent. What do these 26 percent of stocks have in common? They spend most of their time at or near all-time highs.

Check your mutual fund holdings and see if your retirement-account mutual fund managers have been buying Intel, Dell, Microsoft, and other leaders of the past. It guarantees underperformance. Then again, if your mutual fund manager is constantly outperforming the indexes, he or she is likely trend following in a good market and/or making huge bets in a small group of stocks and betting correctly. That outperformance rarely lasts. You can't be lazy with allocating money to active portfolio managers.

Analysts Are No Better—Major Media and Magazines Too

It's not just the TV that you need to shut off—it's the constant flow of research that crosses your desk. If you have a brokerage account and an e-mail account, you know what I mean. You are getting hammered with on-line and institutional research. For example, do you really need a thick research report about the state of the housing industry to tell you what you already know? Can you not drive around town four times a year to get a read on the local real estate market? That is a rhetorical question, by the way. Is the number of homes for sale increasing or decreasing? Are the malls busier or slower than last year? Is a certain restaurant or retail chain popping up all over town, and, more importantly, is it crowded?

In early 2008, JPMorgan released its 312-page state-of-the-Internet report. They declared that Internet stocks would outperform the general market in 2008. By the end of January, the S&P had endured its worst January in history. Google was down 30 percent. My point: These reports will not make you a better investor, so relax. The only takeaway from that 312-page report is that analysts are making good use of their interns. No one is more bullish than I on the Internet, but c'mon—312 pages of research that was proved worthless in two weeks? I can't imagine reading a 312-page report telling me what I already know—that the Internet is likely a 100-year bull market. I don't care about 2008 because, as I mentioned already, returns are not linear.

In January 2008, *Time* magazine chose Vladimir Putin for the cover of their very thinned down issue (advertisers are moving away from print to on-line) as Man of the Year after Russia has already been a stock market darling for ten years. One thing is true from the bull market of 2003–2007: Russia was one of the biggest benefactors. The *Time* cover story was, in effect, old news. If you had been following price and all-time highs, the Russian exchanges, with their heavy weighting of natural resource stocks, had been trending in all-time-high country for four years. Russia had actually been in a straight uptrend since 1998 and hit all-time highs as a country back in 2003. Jumping on the bandwagon after ten years of big gains from magazine hype is not exactly the best effort at trend following.

Magazines are anxiety producing in other ways. Once you've fired up a subscription, the issues keeps coming whether you like it or not, and they just pile up. You feel that you have to read them, as if you may be missing something. If magazines and newspapers are piling up in your home or office, if TV shows are going unwatched because you are backed up on TiVo, now's the time to take control! Cancel your subscriptions. Turn off the TV and skip the TiVo. Free yourself of the noise and anxiety. Investing can be complicated, but I choose to keep it simple. You should too.

Financial Web versus Television

Who should you trust among the many financial commentators and experts that are feeding you conflicting and confusing information? You can't interact with the host or with the owners. Remember, it's a one-way medium.

On the Web, though, you can interact with the authors and find links that allow you to quickly find sources of information; there is a path to follow. If experts on the Internet are not linking, that's a clue that they prefer to follow the one-way-communication model of TV. But if they are giving you the sources from which they are forming their opinions, you can go follow that chain of links, ideas, and opinions in order to develop confidence in their opinions or discount them. People who ask for your trust should disclose, disclose, disclose. You will get much more of that from blogs and the Web. I guarantee that your investing results will improve without news and business television as part of your diet.

The Market Is a Giant Mood Ring

Trend followers are not emotional; they just follow price. Stock prices are driven by moods, not just fundamentals. Americans are generally optimistic, and that is reflected in the long-term charts of the Dow Industrials and the S&P, but we do get overexcited and underexcited at times.

The market was super-excited in 1999 and 2000. We all had a new toy then: the Internet. Companies were building a global information railroad to connect people. The First Transcontinental Railroad, 1,777 miles of track from Omaha to Sacramento, took seven years to construct after a decades-long movement to get it built. Building the infrastructure that supports the Internet was explosive in comparison. The euphoric feeling showed up in the form of stocks such as Cisco, Lucent, Nortel, Qwest, and World-Com—in other words, all the people who were laying the "tracks." If you were part of the Internet investing "irrational exuberance" during the late 1990s, the paper gains were gigantic. Unfortunately, euphoria breeds complacency, and investors without an exit and money-management plans paid the price when the dot-coms crashed.

I believe it is better to be optimistic than pessimistic, but markets turn, trends end, and moods change. When they do, the exit door closes fast. A lot of stock market gains get erased when the mood changes and/or trends end due to market- or company-specific changes. Investing is a business, not a game. For trend followers, if you follow certain money-management rules, the inevitable periods of losses follow *big* gains. With proper money

management, you will be way ahead over the long run (be sure to
read Chapter 5).

The eighteen-month period preceding and immediately following 9/11 was insanely pessimistic and painful. The market had
been going south every day, and the events 9/11 spurred a major
bottom (the gift of hindsight). The market struggled for the next
six months. But America had had enough, and we weren't going
to take any garbage from anybody. Immediately post-9/11, most
predicted total disaster in the stock market, but, of course, it had
already been a disaster.

Institutions used the week off while the markets were closed
for reallocating money. When the market opened, those investors
without a game plan were squashed. They zigged when they should
have zagged. They pulled money out. It felt good, but when do you
get back in? Who rings that bell for you?

The president was given free rein and that started a defense
spending trend. The truth is, our anger set off some insanely profitable trends. Mood once again was a major factor in the stock market. A few years later, just before the United States invaded Iraq,
even though there was talk that it would take seven days to win
the war, the market was spooked as always from the uncertainty.
As the first bomb hit Baghdad, the stock market bottomed. After
the statue of Saddam Hussein came down, the market went pretty
much straight up for three years.

By 2006 we had a president who (according to polls) didn't care
what the country thought and estimates that the war would ultimately cost trillions of dollars. America was also struggling with
drugs, obesity, crime, gas prices, and crumbling infrastructure. And
yet the market had an amazing run. At a time that seemed like
complete chaos, things turned positive in the market.

You have moods that will affect your investing as well. Your own
euphoria or panic can lead you to debate with yourself why you
should or shouldn't take some action. If you had been driven by the
news and by moods during 2005 and 2006, you would say, "Well, I

shouldn't buy stocks because we are going to hell in a hand basket."
If you were watching CNN and Fox, you might have decided that
our civilization had ended. But those were monster years for global
stock markets.

Trends Are Starting and Ending All the Time

In March 2000, the NASDAQ crash began. The bears were calling for Dow 4,000. Even CNBC ratings were in a downward spiral (always a silver lining). But despite all the doom and gloom,
the American real estate market entered a gigantic boom period
and housing stocks replaced Internet stocks as "can't miss" investments.

In 2006, the housing boom ended and the doomsayers returned.
If you were watching all-time highs, you would have noticed
China's market, solar stocks, and thousands of other securities hit-
ting all-time highs.

In January 2008, stocks and indexes from around the world were
having their worst January on record. But from this wreckage, new
leadership will be spawned. The strength will show itself in the one
place it always does in the stock market: on the all-time high list
(check out Chapter 3).

Few know that despite the oil boom, which has sent oil flying
past $100 a barrel, Saudi Arabia's stock market has dropped 70
percent. If you blindly attach oil with Saudi Arabian wealth, your
stock portfolio has crashed. Investing is not that simple.

We are living in the middle of a massive globalization trend,
a shrinking world in which countries such as India, China, Brazil, Korea, and Russia are more involved in the world economy,
bringing millions and millions of new middle-class people to the
consumption marketplace. As they taste wealth and thirst for more,
they have set off trends. Oil, agriculture, and other commodity
stocks have boomed as a result.

Some would argue that railroads were the last great trend because they shrank the world, but the telecom bubble has created what is becoming a lasting railroad—a global network of information—and there has never been anything like it.

The best thing about this information trend is how difficult it is to value. Information leads to knowledge, which leads to wealth. This leads to new power structures. Google replaces Microsoft, online sales beat mall sales, and a man from China is now the richest man in the world. Information and the search for it is the driver of all great booms. That is why we are in the midst of the biggest, longest-lasting boom in history.

Within those global trends, or simply larger trends, other trends exist on a product scale. You must keep your eyes and ears open for the next "something" that captures the attention of consumers. Time is being compressed from this technology boom. Legitimate billion-dollar businesses are being built much faster. There are no sales boundaries, so, believe it or not, this time it is different.

Products in turn create trends around them. Companies other than Apple created a billion-dollar industry making products for the iPod. Just as nothing is static over the course of your own life and trends are starting and stopping all the time, the same thing happens in product cycles—they begin, they peak, and they end. Certain trends last longer than others and those are the ones that we all want to catch. You won't know it until you are in the game, but if you invest long enough, I guarantee you will hit one out of the park.

Forget Perfection—Just Get Started

There are approximately 12,000 actively traded stocks on the U.S. stock exchanges alone. There are 4,000 common stocks with a market cap of at least $300 million and that trade at least $1 million per day in average volume. You need to find just a few great stocks from this list of 4,000 (which is growing all the time) to become a successful investor. Can you guess the greatest-performing NASDAQ stock of all time?

It's not Dell, Microsoft, Intel, or Google. It's Hansen's (HANS), a fruit-juice and energy-drink distributor. After hitting an all-time high in May 2004, the stock rose 2,571 percent at a compounded annual growth rate of 140 percent. I will show you how to find the cream of the crop. Your job is to keep the noise and negative thinking at bay.

Small Is Big and Less Is More

Two ideas—"Small is big" and "Less is more"—are the foundation of my investing philosophy and the philosophy that fueled my creation of Wallstrip.com. Information, social leverage (networking), and software allow us to create more with less. I will delve deeper into this in Chapters 9 and 10.

Investors have never before had so much power. We have access to an enormous amount of information and the means to receive it at our fingertips. We can choose what information we want to receive, choose where and when to receive it, and have it delivered to us rather than constantly searching for it. You can tap into the minds of some of the great financial thinkers in the world, who are actively sharing ideas and information with you. All of it is free—everything you need. Furthermore, the costs that you do have, particularly your transaction costs, have come way down over the last few years.

Less is more because, despite the fact that you have all of that power, you are really better off spending less time on your investments. There are only a few highly skilled professionals who should be paying a lot of attention to their investments on a day-to-day basis. You can only follow a certain number of investment ideas at any one time, maybe twenty to thirty, but that is enough. So do less and enjoy the rest of your life.

Most importantly, do less transacting! You should always be

trying to reduce your transaction costs, which will eat away at your returns. While those costs have been coming down, there is still no free lunch. Lower cost generally means lower service, so there is always some price to be paid. Processing trades and transactions also has a mental cost, a tax cost, and a management cost. Only those few highly skilled professionals should be transacting often. You can do less reading because you can pick the brains of smart, experienced people on the Internet. There is a perfect storm of available knowledge and information available to you on the Web. Tap into it! I will show you how to make the most of it in Chapters 3 and 4.

Bubble—I Got Your Bubble Right Here!

They say that comedy is tragedy plus time. No amount of time heals losses in the stock market. It's never funny and you never feel better. If you do, you don't respect money.

We all have our bubble stories. Mine is CarsDirect.com. I guess we could all insert a name in front of a .com. It was late 1999 and I, like every other hedge fund and mutual fund, was killing it. A friend of a friend who had an uncle who was owed a favor by a banker called me. I could get a piece of CarsDirect.com. It was a sure thing, because Bill Gross of Idealabs was behind it and he was the brains behind Search and EToys.com. They would be public within ninety days of my investment. The term "Booyah" had not been coined by Cramer yet, but I am pretty sure that's what I said.

Long story short, I was in. I mean it was an uncle's banker of a friend of a friend. *Due diligence was for underperformers!* (In fact, that should be printed on a T-shirt line that I think I'm going to start.) In any event, I don't think my wire had hit the other side yet when the NASDAQ peaked over 5,000 that day. The good news was that the company had raised nearly $1 billion from other putzes like me and they could survive awhile. The bad news was that we were all still indeed putzes for investing. CarsDirect.com was created with the genius model of selling cars on-line at a loss. We, of course, could make it up in volume, which, during a bubble, sounds like "We have a cool URL [.com domain] and will get this pig public before others realize we have no idea what to do with $1 billion."

Here is the good part now—at least for me.

In order for the glorious right to own my CarsDirect.com gold mine of a "series Q" pre-IPO home run, I had to buy some shares in Viva.com! Of course that did not matter, for, as you know, due diligence was for underperformers.

Basically, I had the privilege of funding two overpriced ideas.

As luck would have it, my investment in Viva.com! turned out to be a wonderful investment. Fantastic management and a new business plan bailed me out. A smart purchase of the domain name Rent.com came first. Management of Rent.com treated their investors' money like gold, adapted to the post-nuclear tech market of 2001, and by 2005 built a very profitable model. They sold to eBay for an incredible price—over $400 million.

CarsDirect.com became part of a lead-generation business called Internet Brands and managed to get public in 2007 (NASD: INET). Even after going public in 2007, my investment had lost over 80 percent of its value. I did not deserve even that from this greed-based investment.

I guess the real moral of the story is that we are all smart in bull markets. So always try to remember that, because a bear market is around the corner for us all.

My Trading Was Not Any Better

When I was trading alongside my genius private investments, I wanted to beat the market on a daily basis. That can be a really sexy drug, and for five or six years I was addicted to it. I was at it from five in the morning until ten at night. I never left it alone. I didn't make appointments or take calls. All I did was trade and watch the screen. Then I burned out, and I looked at my results and they just didn't jibe with the work I did: It wasn't worth the cost. Even the best traders are right barely 50 percent of the time. Who wants to be in that business? I decided not me!

Don't Listen to the Old Rules—Here Are the "New Rules"

One cable TV show segment that I really enjoy is Bill Maher's "New Rules" segment from his weekly HBO show, *Politically Incorrect*. Here are some of my favorites:

> *New Rule: You don't have to recall things that would make people sick anyway. General Mills has recalled five million Jeno's frozen pizzas because they might be contaminated with e. coli. Couldn't they just as easily say they're recalling five million strains of e. coli because they might be contaminated with Jeno's pizza? I mean, what's the difference? One gives you stomach cramps and diarrhea, and the other is e. coli!*

> *New Rule: If America's richest one-percent are now so rich that even a five-star hotel isn't good enough, it's time to bring back the guillotine.*

Bill is not for everybody, but this segment stands for challenging the ridiculous and thinking creatively. He reads headlines inside out and upside down. Those traits have also made the Drudge Report one of highest-trafficked Internet news sites and made Jon Stewart and Stephen Colbert household names.

In some ways, like Bill Maher, Wallstrip.com proved that in today's world the old rules do not apply. Big changes are at hand in media. Just a few years ago, if you wanted to create something like Wallstrip.com you had to have major connections to money and media. Now you need bandwidth, a video camera, and a good idea.

The same is true of finding trends. We are living in a "connected" world where a product can be released in Oregon and a hundred thousand people can be using the product in Indonesia two weeks later. The world has "shrunk." Growth potential and opportunities have exploded to a point where God could not value companies like Apple, Research In Motion, and Google. If God can't value them, why are you going to trust Goldman Sachs or anyone else? The research rules and models of the past have been stretched and broken apart. Why bother spending a nickel of your time worrying about it? Turn off the TV and take control.

To-Do List

1. Turn off your TV to eliminate noise and anxiety about investing in stocks.

2. Forget the blame game. You are in control.

3. Opinions are like assholes . . .

4. Stay open minded and avoid price targets.

5. Invest—just start!

6. Focus on opportunities and always be mindful of doing less.

CHAPTER 2

Trend Following Works

In order to maximize your profits (let them run), you must be willing to give some of them back.

—Van K. Tharp

We spend fortunes as consumers buying goods that are a part of "hot" trends. We *should* also focus on putting money back in our pockets off these same trends. The best way to do this is through stock ownership—not just any stock ownership, but the best of breed, as in the fastest-growing companies in the world. The stock market in the United States is our greatest symbol of capitalism. Yes, your money can disappear, but you are in control. Yes, the "suits" (investment banks) want to put their hands in your pocket, but you have the ultimate power over the buy-and-sell decisions. Investing in the stock market is not free, but it's getting pretty close as technology and competition have lowered the costs of transactions to nearly nil.

Yet despite the great advances in technology, Wall Street has been able to perform the same marketing and distributing shenanigans for over 100 years. Investors just never seem to learn that Wall Street's end game is to put the shares of a few into the hands of many. Unfortunately, they will do this until the end of time and they will teach it globally. The great news is that *you* can avoid this end game. At the very least, this book will show you how to rid

Enron, subprime mortgage, homebuilding, and WorldComs from your stock and investment statements long before they become disasters.

Trending stocks are often referred to in the media as "momentum stocks." *Trend* is a word associated with products and markets, but rarely with individual stocks. I think the term "momentum" has actually helped investors who follow this strategy, as it scares the average investor and has kept trend-following disciples to a minimum. But it's changing fast. The media would lead you to believe that momentum trading is a fool's game and that the key to success in the market is buying low and selling high. You will not find that same advice here. I will challenge the media and the accepted trading and investing terms throughout this book.

Trend Following: My First Taste

I was introduced to trend following in 2002. The stock market was entering its third year in the dumps and I was worn out. I was managing my hedge fund and looking for ways to put money to work. My two associates, Cole and Eric (now Blackstar Fund founders), had been studying hundreds of strategies for one they could get excited about. They approached me with trend followers, specifically Salem Abraham, a trend follower with an amazing track record.

Classic trend followers use futures to trade hundreds of markets, including gold, currencies, grains, oil, and stock market futures. They go both long and short. Leverage was not something I fully understood, but I quickly learned the good and the bad. From the moment I allocated money to Salem, his returns skyrocketed. Of course, that was the worst thing that could have happened to someone like me. It was like going to a casino and winning for the first few nights—you think the casino *pays you*. Sadly, it does not. I allocated more money to trend managers, including Fall River Capital. The gains continued.

In 2004, thinking that trend guys only made money, I was recommending the strategy to everybody. Let's just say the timing was bad. I had bought into the additional belief that trading more markets meant greater diversification. Let's just say *Oy* (sometimes all markets are correlated). The period that ensued was one of the worst ever for trend followers. Fall River went into a straight-down 50 percent spiral. I was the proverbial deer in the headlights. The "book" on trend following said you should allocate to trend followers when they were losing money. If I had, I would have been the only one! They were losing money fast and the supposed "smart money" (institutions) were pulling money faster than me. For the most part, though, I stayed the course.

Flash forward to 2008, and even Fall River has recovered from those massive losses. Despite the ups and downs, I have been intrigued by the strategy from the beginning. In other words, that original punishment did not shake the trend-following bug from my system. The truth is, trend following worked. It was not perfect, but I was sure there was a way to profit consistently.

The Incredible Power of Trending and Momentum Stocks

One of the biggest proponents of trend investing is the founder of *Investor's Business Daily* (IBD), William O'Neil. O'Neil was building stocks and market databases long before most, and, more importantly, he was organizing and delivering the data in ways that smart investors enjoyed. Furthermore, he continues to be the innovator in the delivery of information. His financial newspaper continues to evolve and to add features for most trend investors.

Data may become a commodity as we enter the next decade, but how businesses organize, present, market, and deliver it remains the secret sauce. The weekend edition of *Investor's Business Daily* (IBD) is my most regular old-media read. I love the way it organizes the strongest stocks in the market, and their market page gives a great snapshot of the overall health of the stock market. Newspapers have been in a slow death march since the Internet began, but the IBD remains an example of a winner inside a losing trend. You should get used to reading it as well, in order to get a feel for what stocks and industries are strongest.

Take a look at the following chart, which was put together by my friend Eddy Elfenbein, who writes one of my favorite stock and market blogs, www.crossingwallstreet.com:

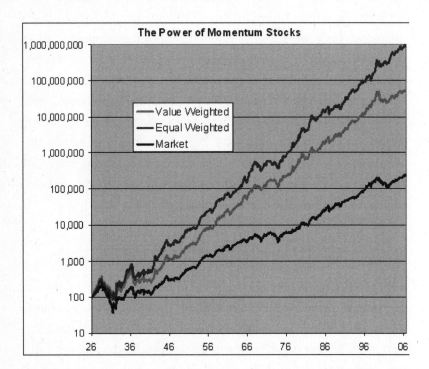

The chart shows you how the top 10 percent of momentum stocks have done against the top 10 percent of book value, price and earnings ratio, dividend yield, and price-to-cash flow. It's not even close.

Don't just believe Eddy and me. The London Business School recently declared the following:

"Momentum, or the tendency for stock returns to trend in the same direction, is a major puzzle," the LBS three comment.

"In well-functioning markets, it should not be possible to make money from the naïve strategy of simply buying winners and selling losers. Yet there is extensive evidence that momentum profits have been large and pervasive."

The numbers certainly back up the claim. In one of LBS's studies, which analysed all fully-listed stocks between 1955 and 2007, the shares which had outperformed the market most in the previous 12 months went on to generate an annualised return of 18.3pc while the market's worst laggards rose by 6.8pc on average.

Is the Stock Market Efficient?

Based on what you have read so far, you know my answer.

The market is as efficient as my forty-year-old bowels—once in a while. Yet open up most stock and market books, and they will talk about the argument of efficient markets. That argument won't make you money. If you have *real* money on the line, the only thing that matters is being right. If you don't believe me, take it from someone else, like Jesse Livermore, the fabled trader of *Reminiscences of a Stock Operator* (one of my favorite books):

It takes a man a long time to learn all the lessons of all his mistakes. They say there are two sides to everything. But there is only one side to the stock market; and it is not the bull side or the bear side, but the right side. It took me longer to get that general principle fixed firmly in my mind than it did most of the more technical phases of the game of stock speculation.

Stock prices are a combination of actual financials, supply, demand, perception, and moods. If the market were efficient, the problems at Enron and WorldCom would have been predicted after the first hint of a problem. Instead, the stocks slowly made their way to zero. If you call that efficient, I guess I am wrong.

During the Internet bubble and all periods of increased speculation, stocks screamed higher with no revenues and no fundamentals. Mood trumped financials. Many smart people went broke being right about Yahoo and Amazon being overvalued. A stock could go from an overvalued amount of $260 to $1,000 before it stops and reverses. In effect, you could eventually be right and go bust on the way. Today it is Chinese stocks and solar stocks. With solar stocks, there is not nearly enough supply of stock to satiate the giddiness. Investors are in love with anything solar. There are probably ten legitimate public companies right now and just a few mutual funds could own the whole solar float of available public shares. First Solar and the rest of the solar gang would make better shorts when they are completely broken. For First Solar (NASD : FSLR), that could be 100 points higher and twelve months from this time, for all I or anybody knows. The homebuilders were great shorts when they were down 50 percent from their all-time highs. Shit, they have been good shorts down 70 percent.

Trending Stocks Are the Hardest to Value: That's Great News

By definition, securities that are trending are difficult to value. The stock market is a discounting mechanism, which means that stocks that are moving up or down in trends cannot be properly valued. Otherwise, they would move in tight sideways ranges. Trending stocks are an investor's best place to make money. The great companies that will make three to even twenty times your money in the stock market are by nature very challenging to value. The reams of numbers that analysts spend thousands of hours on do not give them an edge. Following trends gives you the ability to put your money in only the best stocks in the market, which are essentially those that are the hardest to value.

Here's Why

The sheer amount of metrics and market potential has recently expanded, and Wall Street research has not kept up with the power and leverage obtained from the "flat" or "shrinking" world. Rail-roads, ships, airplanes, and the Internet have shrunk the globe to a point where information is always accessible, products can be bought and sold at any time from anywhere, and business opportunities are endless. This global customer base provides new opportunities for trends to start. While the world was awash in capital (that trend is in trouble in early 2008), stock markets around the world were in vogue. China, India, Russia, Mexico, and Brazil are getting their first tastes of wealth, and they like it. Markets will always correct, but the new markets are built. Electronic exchange traded funds (ETFs) have been accepted, and as they proliferate, you have access to global and sector diversification. Finally, technology has created a twenty-four-hour electronic exchange, which has further helped to push the boundaries of free markets, trading, and global wealth.

How Stock Markets Really Work: Scarcity

First things first: Nothing lasts forever. Don't be naive. The law of large numbers catches up with all companies and will, in turn, always catch up to individual stocks and hot sectors. If not, Wall Street supply will catch up with runaway markets and stocks. Just as great white sharks are perfect killing machines, investment banks, analysts, and brokers are the perfect supply-and-distribution machines. They solve excessive stock-demand problems with stock—lots and lots of stock. You must understand how the stock market works to understand that nothing can go on forever. It is why a staggering 1 of 3 stocks in the public market eventually decline 75 percent or more from their IPO prices (see the chart in Chapter 1).

When a company is hot, two things can happen: management calls a banker or a banker calls management. At this point, the end game of stock supply is set in motion. You should know that we as public or common shareholders are the last in line, at the bottom of the totem pole. We are being sold something: buyer beware. Stocks are not toys. Investing is not a game. The odds are stacked against you to *riding* the eventual winners, even if you do a great job finding them.

Here are the players on the road to you holding common stock:

1. The Founder(s)/ Entrepreneur(s)
2. The Company/Employees
3. The Bankers
4. The Brokers
5. The Analysts
6. The Mutual Funds and Hedge Funds—The Institutions
7. The Media (Television, Newspapers, Magazines, Blogs)
8. The Regulatory Agencies—SEC, NASD
9. The Common Shareholder—You and Me!

If you think this motley group of people with conflicting interests can make an efficient market, you are deluded. You have forces pulling to make things inefficient and forces pulling (hoping) to make things efficient. The only thing random here is the chance that things *could* be efficient. Markets are chaotic. The time frame in which you look at the market makes a big difference. Generally, the longer the time frame, at least with markets as a whole, the smoother the price movements. Small investors have an advantage by recognizing the chaos and looking for longer-term big-picture ideas.

A simple understanding of supply and demand is all it takes. A great company's stock is scarce. There are millions of potential customers for both the product and the stock of fast-growing companies and only a limited supply. Economics 101: Increased demand and limited supply equals price appreciation. There are 20,000-plus institutions looking to own the best companies, but there is only one Chipotle, Apple, or Research In Motion. Trends persist because you cannot time the supply-and-demand issue. Owning a second-rate Mexican food chain is not the same as owning Chipotle. Owning Dell is not the same as owning Apple. Take advantage of that. Products get created and released; the same with companies. Some are accepted by the public market for their products and financial performance, and some are not. Those that work show themselves in price via persistent all-time highs. Wall Street's goal is to print as much paper (that's what banks manufacture) to satisfy the most people at the exact wrong time. All trends end the same way—too many shares distributed to far too many people. The scarcity problem is solved—usually as a company nears the end of its growth cycle.

Housing Market Case Study

The housing bubble is an amazing, sad, and, unfortunately, painful lesson in scarcity and the distribution machine that is Wall Street. It is also a case study in greed and fear. In 2002, born out of low interest rates and a flood of cheap money and credit into the U.S. economy, homebuilding stocks exploded. They did so while the stock market averages were in the doldrums, while Internet stocks were crashed, and venture capital investing was non-existent. Many factors converged at once to create extra demand for homes and homebuilder stocks.

As usual, Wall Street was there to solve the demand problem, print stock, do secondary offerings, and get the media into a frenzy at exactly the wrong time. I started writing the case study back in February of 2007 (Wall Street set this case study in motion when housing stocks first broke out to new highs in 2002). The title of my post at the time was "Homebuilders: The New Value Trap."

Here is what I wrote:

Five years from now when the homebuilding stocks are 20–30 percent lower and marking time, small investors will all own shares in what the institutions have distributed to them since mid 2006. The companies are not crap and they won't be in 5 years, but the stocks will be value traps. Victims of a badly ended trend where the stocks were overowned and overhyped. It is no one person's fault, it is just the way Wall Street works. They are just not real growth stocks. Nothing was different this time and no particular CEO or management team will be totally immune.

The industry will continue to go out of favor with Mutual Funds. That does not mean you should sell your home or get bearish on the world. Hundreds of new trends have been emerging since the homebuilders peaked last spring.

Do not over think it and get sucked into buying value. That's for Warren Buffett and a select few, great value managers.

Housing stocks, not housing as a business in general, are done. Housing is cyclical, always has been, always will be. You CAN overbuild, just like you can make too much capacity for semiconductors—we did that in 1999. With homebuilders, leverage sped things up.

I never tried to call a top in housing, but definitely warned that it would get worse after they had already fallen 50 percent back in February of 2007. I followed up repeatedly. I guess that's why the permabears "disgust" me so. As if calling a top makes you a special gifted market person. I guess I was wrong about housing stocks being a value trap way back when. They never made it to value, just straight to bankruptcy. Owning them now is not for anyone other than forensic accountants who have a crystal ball into The Fed and lenders tolerance or for penny stock speculators.

At the beginning of 2008, Jeff Matthews (www.jeffmatthewsis notmakingthisup.blogspot.com) did a great look back at his housing "top" call. Jeff is not scared of shorting on the way up. That's why I would *never* act on his posts. I am not wired, nor do I have deep enough pockets, to bet against the crowd. But he has seen all the cycles. We get to read Jeff's missives for *free*. You just need to know how to read them. Here is my favorite part of the blog post on the housing industry:

> *I bought* Time *magazine today for the first time since . . . probably since 9/11, when I bought every newspaper and magazine available with a cover story on the World Trade Center attacks. The relevance of a weekly "news magazine" these days is, after all, right up there with "Book-of-the-Month" clubs and the Sears Catalogue.*
>
> *Nevertheless, I bought this new issue of* Time *magazine because the front cover is titled "Home Sweet Home" (stamped in large letters, the "S" converted into a Dollar sign) with an illustration showing a man covetously hugging a house. The sub-title reads: "Why we're going gaga over real estate."*
>
> *I bought it, quite simply, because this* Time *magazine is as good a "cover story" kind of market-mania, surely-we-are-approaching-a-top indicator as I have ever seen. (See jeffmatthewsisnotmakingthisup.blogspot.com/Jeff Matthews)*

If you had been excited reading Jeff's great post in June of 2005 and sold all your housing stocks and even shorted, you would have been right, just a little early.

At the time when I am finishing this book (June 2008), both China and solar are case studies in waiting. It's the exact same scenario. Wall Street is increasing the supply of paper to satisfy demand. Timing when supply overtakes demand is a fool's game, but it will happen. Both trends will end the same way, but you don't need to predict when, just avoid being the person holding the shares once it is clear the trend has run its course.

How Do You Look at the World?

Take a look at the picture below. Is the glass half full or half empty?

If you answered half full, you are lucky, positive, and on the right track. If you believe it is half empty, you need to change the way you look at the world—at least as it relates to investing. People who look at the glass as half full help to make the markets. Don't get me wrong—that doesn't mean it is a perfect perspective. In 2000, too many people were looking at the glass as half full, and that led to horrific price declines. As you learn and if you embrace trend investing, you will welcome the naysayers and no longer fear them. You will get better at recognizing patterns in the stock market and patterns of investor behavior. You will do this without spending long hours studying stock charts and fundamentals.

Does Momentum Trump the Market?

If you see the glass as half empty, the headlines would have been wonderful for you in 2007. The year 2007 was by no means a special year with respect to U.S. stock market returns (The S&P ended the year up 3.5 percent). The war in Iraq did not dominate the headlines as much as in 2006, but it continued nonetheless. Oil was a hair shy of $100, the U.S. dollar was at all-time lows against a basket of global currencies, gold was at twenty-five-year highs, and there was a housing crash and a credit crunch, forcing emergency federal-reserve actions. Despite the nasty headlines, all the U.S. major market averages were up for the year. Many stocks and sectors experienced huge gains in 2007, stocks that I mentioned in Chapter 1 that I covered in length on my blog in 2006 and 2007.

So who gets rewarded? Five percent of stocks appreciated by more than 1,000 percent between 1983 and 2006, and 5 percent appreciated between 500 and 1,000 percent. Fifty percent had a negative return, and an astounding 33 percent, or 1 out of every 3 stocks, lost at least 75 percent of their value. According to the stock data compiled by my friends at Blackstar, a handful of stocks are responsible for the bulk of the index gains. Just a simple buy-and-hold strategy is not as simple as it sounds. Selling is an important part of the investment puzzle—likely the most important.

Does Trend Following Work in Reverse?

If 1 out of 3 stocks drop 75 percent, trend following in reverse must be like shooting fish in a barrel! I wish. I have yet to see someone, anyone, make money by consistently shorting stocks despite the amazing failure rate of stocks. If I had discovered the secret stock-market formula to making money *all* the time, *guaranteed*, I would be making money off it, not sharing the playbook with the masses.

Trend following to the upside gives me an edge and improves my quality of life, and that's what I want to pass on. Furthermore, looking at the world with a "glass is half empty" attitude makes your investing life that much harder. My friend Tim Knight, based in California, is a successful investor and entrepreneur. He has a detailed "bearish" blog at www.slopeofhope.com. I am always amazed at the work-to-stress ratio he employs to follow the stock market. And in my opinion, most of the time his writing sounds like he has been tortured by the stock market. But Tim is wired for it. He even explains on his blog why a person should *not* be a bear:

(1) The whole world is against you. From the investment banks, to CNBC, to Jim Cramer, to the brokerage houses, everyone on the planet wants the market to go up forever. There is a huge, huge, huge vested interest in the markets going skyward for all eternity.

(2) No one gets rich being a bear. Fortunes like Warren Buffett's are made by investing in stocks that reap multi-thousand percent gains or more. There is no one on the Forbes 400 who got there by being a bear.

Tim's bearish arguments are often insightful, and while I respect his integrity and tenacity in the face of the odds, I feel he is swimming upstream. No matter how intelligent he may be (and he is), I sense that he has to work that much harder to end up in the same place as optimistic, long-term positive thinkers. I will spend little time in this book discussing the merits and intricacies of short selling. That may seem silly to some, since 1 of 3 stocks make the ultimate trip to zero. My problem is that I really don't know a rich short seller. I don't know of a dedicated short seller who wants to share with me—or anyone, for that matter—the seemingly great business of betting against stocks. I read Tim for his honesty, and I have learned how to read him.

The statistical takeaway from Eric's chart and research is that if you are not extremely careful, you will own many stocks in your investing career on their way to 75 percent losses. Whether Tim knows the statistics or not, this is what he understands. It is just so damn hard to do this profitably. What really amazes me is how little time is spent on the most important part of portfolio management: managing losses so they you don't hold stocks on the way to being the bad statistics from Eric's chart.

The great news is that I will show you how to find the 10 percent of stocks that increase over 500 percent in their lifetimes. I will also show you how to recognize stocks that are on their way to 75 percent losses. You can use www.howardlindzon.com and www. wallstrip.com for idea generation and support, but ultimately you have to control your hard-earned or inherited money, and it is you who must take responsibility for shrinking it or growing it.

To-Do List

1. There is no perfect strategy, but you *must* be willing to give back profits to ride trends.

2. Wall Street's goal is to take shares from the few and distribute them to the many—don't forget this. Wall Street is not an exclusive enclave for the wealthy.

3. The fastest-growing stocks are hard to value, and that is good.

4. Momentum is a viable strategy and trend following works.

5. Trend following works in reverse as well—1 out of 3 stocks drops 75 percent. Money management always rules the day!

6. There are no Fortune 500 short sellers, so do what you can to keep a positive attitude. Read short sellers' blogs carefully.

CHAPTER 3

Finding Trends

You can't handle the truth!

—*A Few Good Men*

The All-Time-High List: Embrace It

My secret formula is hereby revealed.

I know you want more and I would be happy to give it to you, but that's how I start and end my search for stocks. All the great stocks show up here, so why look anywhere else? The truth is, you would have participated in RailroadMania, NiftyFifty-mania, MicrosoftMania, YahooMania, OilMania, and GoogleMania if only you had been watching the all-time-high lists. With the proliferation of inverse ETFs, you would have also participated in CreditCrunchMania as financial and real estate stocks plummeted in 2007 and 2008.

I remember when we profiled Google on Wallstrip in October 2006, after the infamous YouTube acquisition of $1.6 billion. The "man on the street" was aghast at GoogleMania. People couldn't believe how overvalued Google was at $400. They preferred Yahoo and Microsoft because they were cheaper! Google continued on to $700—not a home run, but a great one-year return and long-term capital gain for those willing to follow price and all-time highs. I wrote this following our show back in October 2006:

It's happening. Watch the Wallstrip Google video again. The "man on the street" does not believe. The "man on the street" does not own Google. They own Yahoo and Microsoft. They own 500 shares, 100 shares, 10 shares of that crap.

Don't worry—Google paper will be crap as well—just not yet.

It is the same f@#cking game played over and over by Wall Street. IT IS CALLED DISTRIBUTION. It takes time. When Wall Street gets hold of a beauty like Google, they take their sweet time distributing it one share at a time to every last believer in the story. See—Intel, Microsoft, Dell and Yahoo. Could take 15 years or three. The Google stock distribution game has just begun.

It is the normal complaints I am hearing again—stock is too high, market cap is ridiculous, shares are too expensive, too many acquisitions, I should have bought at $162, should have bought on the pullback to $320 . . .

In the meantime, everyone owns Yahoo and Microsoft—stock is too low, market cap and PE are reasonable, it's cheap relative to Google, I can always double down cheaper because it's already so low. OY!

In summary, if you want to make money trend following, you need to stop hating the manias and learn to *embrace them*. There are always trends at work in the stock market. If you watch the all-time-high list, you will be looking at opportunities from a database of companies into which money is flowing *today*.

Invest in Healthy Markets for Healthy Returns

If the stock market is strong and you have many stocks to choose from on the all-time-high list, your probability of success rises. Don't just look at the Dow Industrials. The Dow is based on thirty stocks and is price weighted. The highest-priced stock has the most influence on the Dow. You did not hear it from me first, but the Dow can go wherever the big money wants it to go for a good period of time—long enough to fool you. Use the broader-based indexes like the S&P 500 or the Wilshire 5000.

My most trusted method to gauge the health of the market is by monitoring the all-time-high lists over a period of time. Price is the greatest predictor, but you need some context. How many all-time highs are there today versus last month, for example? The more the merrier. And with some practice, you won't need to see the indexes. You will just know whether cash is king.

In February of 2008, just a handful of stocks were hitting all-time highs, mainly in biotech, gold, oil, and basic materials. I owned many of them, but my overall positions were light because I do not consider these sectors to be growth areas. Their success implies problems for the real growth stocks. One year earlier there were hundreds of stocks to choose from. We want to be hunting for winners when the leaders are plentiful.

As noted, *Investor's Business Daily* has a great one-page daily summary of the overall markets. I check it at least once a week. Watching the all-time-high list over a period of three to six months will give you a great additional feel as to the overall health of the financial markets. One huge advantage of trend following is the reduced overall workload. It's less taxing on the mind. We all want to make better returns while doing less, so in bad markets, fewer stocks will show up on the new-high list and you will inevitably be doing less. Trust me, it works.

Sideways Is Good!

From my own trading experiences and my reading of the missives of successful traders, timing your entries is not as important as managing your exits. I want to own stocks at all-time highs, but buying stocks as they emerge to all-time highs from longer periods of sideways action is something I try to do. It is more art than science, so managing the position is really the secret sauce.

From monitoring the all-time high list you not only get a feel for the overall market, but you also see the new names emerging over time. As you start seeing the long-term charts of the best stock gainers throughout the book, you will notice the long sideways actions that frequently occur before big gains.

Sharks? Pilot Fish?

I like to use a simple analogy to explain trending stocks at or near all-time highs. Sharks move water and they cannot hide. The pilot fish swim underneath the shark. That's their job, and they are genetically coded to do that. If they venture too far away from the shark, they run the risk of getting lost or eaten. Not a bad life, and I imagine the pilot fish can do some serious trash talking.

Individual investors can learn much from the pilot fish. The financial world is made up of giant institutions, and they are moving money the way sharks move water. Once they start moving money, they can't hide it, so if you are an investor and you are smart, you swim with the giant institutions. You follow them. Closely.

Following the giant institutions as they move money is akin to hiring the best minds in the financial world. Some would argue the term *best*, but in the real world of money and finance, *big* and *best* often go hand in hand. The main reason companies are at all-time highs is that they are performing better than the rest, and influential people, people with knowledge and power, have been buying them. Those people are doing the research for you, and they have the resources and skill to do it better than you possibly could, even if you did have the time. The sharks usually know where a stock is going, and you cannot compete with them over time. Let those smart people work for you and go with the flow.

Finding Trends: An Example

My experience in buying and selling Crocs is a perfect example of how I approach finding, riding, and getting off trends. In October

2006, I noticed that Crocs' stock had hit an all-time high. I found it the same way I am telling you to find stocks, by monitoring the daily list of all-time highs. Lots of stocks were breaking out. Crocs are those ugly rubber shoes with holes in them, the ones that look like a hollowed-out football for your feet.

Here is what I wrote in October 2006:

I wear the Crocs knockoffs that my friends at Lifestyle Brands in Toronto manufacture and sell like crazy. This is the most comfortable shoe to ever grace my feet. Since I buy new highs . . . I am intrigued. Crocs is a BILLION dollar company already—HOW? Does it have legs (feet for that matter)? What is the catalyst for this relative start-up already on fire?

First off, they have been smart about dealing with knockoffs— SETTLE. Focus on the road and business ahead. Want real proof how well they are executing—go visit their bad ass website. Go check out Flickr and search CROX. Check out the Google term "Crocs." Actually, Googling "Crocs" got me thinking. Private Label shoes. Nike has done it on their website and my nephew sleeps with his self-designed shoe (Nobody innovates better than Nike). I expect CROX to blow up this area with their easy to manufacture shoe.

Long story short—CROX is for real.

Suppose you noticed your friends and neighbors, as well as people at the mall, and maybe even your grandmother, wearing Crocs.

Suppose that you then went to Wallstrip.com, the Internet show and blog that I founded, and read what I wrote about Crocs. Suppose that you had taken my advice and visited Flickr (www.flickr.com), the Web site where people share their photos on-line. There you would have found thousands of pictures of people and their Crocs. A Google search for "Crocs" would have uncovered testimonials from all kinds of people: doctors and chefs, hikers and sailors, hairstylists and seniors just like Granny. Your search would have pointed you to YouTube, a video-sharing site, where you would have seen videos about Crocs. That's right: people making videos about their shoes!

You might also have gone to Google Finance or Yahoo Finance and read about the people who make Crocs, seen their financial statements, visited that bad-ass Web site, and been amazed by the list of thousands of stores that carry Crocs. You might have typed in your zip code, found the store nearest your home, gone there, and asked a few pertinent questions, such as "How are people reacting to Crocs?" and "How fast are they moving off the shelves?"

You might have become convinced that Crocs were a true cultural phenomenon and not just a flash-in-the-pan product. You might have bought a pair of Crocs and loved them. Then you might have bought Crocs (CROX) stock (like I did) at that all-time high. Your friends would have called you crazy. It's an ugly shoe. Your broker might have tried to talk you out of it ticking off the short interest or the high price-earnings ratio. But if you had bought it after our first show, you would have watched it gain close to 300 percent in the next year. If you had followed my blog you would have also captured a big gain as we sold on the way up.

No gain is really a gain until booked. Managing positions so that big winners do not ultimately become losers is extremely important. I will drill down into the mechanics of managing positions—losses and gains—in Chapter 5.

A Trend That Found Me

Some trends really do just hit you on the head. I was taking my kids to McDonald's and we were walking past a restaurant I had never heard about—Chipotle—and people were lined up outside the door. I don't like Mexican food but my daughter does, so she changed her mind about McDonald's and wanted to go to

Chipotle instead. We waited in line about ten minutes and I got myself a burrito.

I had never seen a restaurant like that. I got everything the way I wanted it, everything tasted great, and it was quick. My son didn't like it, but my daughter loved it, and I asked the guy at the cash register, "Who owns Chipotle?" He said, "McDonald's," and I thought, *Rats*. When I got home I looked at McDonald's stock and saw that it was in the twenties, so it was not near an all-time high. I found out Chipotle had only seventy restaurants and McDonald's had thousands, so Chipotle was not going to make a difference to McDonald's stock. But I wrote on my blog that "someone at McDonald's should get a raise for buying that company." (In hindsight, buying McDonald's stock would have been a great decision as well.)

Six or eight months later, after I had been eating at Chipotle once a week with my daughter, I heard that they were doing an IPO. I wrote about it, saying, "It doesn't matter what happens with this IPO. Whatever price it comes out at, it's a buy." I was confident after eating there all that time and seeing how they ran the restaurant, how four people could run an operation like that, and how simple the menu was: burritos, tacos, chips, and salsa. They also did the little things that made eating there a great experience, such as using free-range chicken and keeping the place clean. It was not like a usual fast-food restaurant, but the prices were pretty much the same. Every time I talked to the management they said that the restaurants were doing well, and no matter where I went to a Chipotle, they were busy.

What excited me most was that they were in only a few southwestern states, so they had a lot of opportunity in front of them. America has 300 million people. When you find a chain that is run the way Chipotle is run, and then you see that it is in only a few states, you feel like you really have something. The really nice thing is that Chipotle is a cookie-cutter operation, meaning that they figured out how to run it, so it was just a matter of duplicating the formula. I believed it was a trend I could jump on. When your kid likes it and you like it too, it's an easy decision. You just know that you are going to make money with something like that. When you have that confidence, you can tune out a lot of the noise. When Chipotle came public, I closed my eyes and bought it. The stock nearly tripled in eight months.

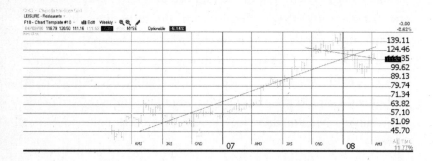

If you missed out on Chipotle, be alert for the next Chipotle and, as I always say, Chipotle may still be "the next" Chipotle. Your opportunities are endless. Do not get bogged down in the ones you missed or the ones where you screwed up. Just keep your eyes open for the next one. If you can be profitable just 50 percent of the time finding stock trends, and if you manage your losses, then you can make money. If you are profitable 60 percent of the time, you will make a lot of money.

Touching the Product: The "Experience"

I must believe that a company and its products fit my style—both my lifestyle and my investing style. Buying and holding stocks is like buying and wearing clothes. Jeans are just pieces of denim, and stocks are just pieces of paper. Learn to look at investing in that way and stay true to your own style. I have too many pairs of jeans that don't fit. I might have bought them because of a great salesperson, the branding, or the fact that I was in a great mood and/or in a rush. I have a closet full of clothes, but only six pairs of pants that I like. So what do I need? I need pants that fit. Buy only green stocks if that fits your style, or only vice stocks, or neither of those. Both stocks and clothes have to fit and make you comfortable. Not all clothes or stocks will work for you, so you have to experiment, maybe try some things on until you find a style that fits your risk profile.

When you have spotted a company on the list of all-time highs that resonates with you and you can understand it, you need to take it further. If you have no experience with the product, you then need to interact with it. If it is Crocs, go to the store that sells them, ask questions, buy a pair and wear them for a while. If it is Chipotle, go eat a burrito. Talk to the employees.

Apple

My encounter with the iPod in 2005 is another good example of how I did some groundwork and experienced the product—and I'm not even a technology person. I have never been comfortable with gadgets, but the iPod resonated with me the first time I picked one up. Then when I went to work out at the health club I would see a few people wearing those white iPod ear buds and I knew in my heart of hearts that within a year or two, nine out of ten people would have those ear buds. I wouldn't buy the stock because it wasn't even close to being at an all-time-high; buying it then would have violated my boundaries.

But I did buy an iPod and was using it, and it just so happened that an Apple Store stood across the street from my office. I found myself in that store all the time, and I noticed how busy it was and how much activity there was around the product. Eventually the stock started moving up and the stronger it got the more confident I became. I did not buy it at twelve dollars a share, the approximate price at the time. I waited until the stock tripled (still not an all-time high), and by then it had already risen to about forty dollars (pre-splits). I could not resist. I felt it in my bones.

It seemed like the craziest time to buy the stock, but it proved to be a really good buy.

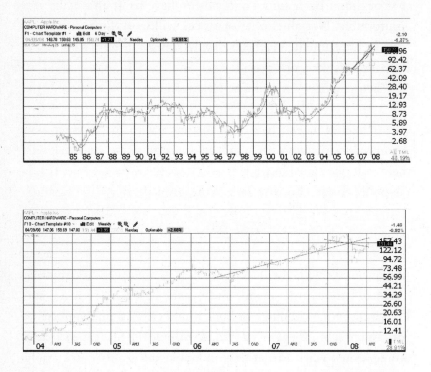

Sure enough, the white ear buds were all over the health club and the stock went up over 400 percent in the next two years. The iPod was a product I used and liked. It came from a place where I shop and was part of the lifestyle that I have adopted. The people around me also used it and liked it. All of those things gave me comfort in the catalyst for the stock. I could shut out the naysayers. I was actually emboldened by them, as they would be fuel for the fire when they finally purchased an Apple product. My investing standpoint was not all that different from my consumer standpoint: I was part of the trend. I was not the first person to buy an iPod or Apple stock, but that didn't mean I couldn't make money.

Try to look at the products you use, enjoy, and promote every day in a different light. You are spending your money on them, but they may also put money back in your pocket. Also, get in the habit of being in tune with which companies are performing best. Over time, the picture will start becoming clearer to you. It is not an overnight revelation, but a process. To begin, you may just grab a piece of paper and list the products you use every day. Then you have to do a little research (Chapter 4). This is not free. People do not just put money out in the street for you. There is some work involved.

I like to be able to touch and feel the products or services of the companies I invest in. It helps me form an opinion. That is why Chipotle, Crocs, and Apple were important for me. I used them and they made my life better, so I figured that they had to be helping other people as well. When you touch a product and it makes you feel like that, then you are more involved and can develop the confidence in a catalyst that allows you to buy the stock and hold it long enough for it to make a difference to your investment returns.

An employee at the Apple Store in Phoenix bought Apple stock, quit his job as a banker, and went to work for Apple so that he could keep in touch with their thinking, strategy, and products. He made several million dollars because he was excited about Apple's products and wanted to stay close to his investment. He had a vision where the company was going and wanted to be a deeper part of it. You don't have to quit your job and go to work for another company; this is an extreme but true example.

For me, the BlackBerry is another product like Crocs, the iPod, and Chipotle. I used my "CrackBerry" sixteen hours a day. If you get your hands around a product like that and it makes your life better, then you're on to something. You have to examine the stock price and market conditions, but that kind of experience is a great starting point.

In February 2008, Apple dropped from $200 to $119. My stop was at $140, so I gave back approximately 30 percent of my gains at the end of this trend. I stuck to my sell discipline (Chapter 5). It hurt to sell my favorite stock and company of three years, but if I was not trend following I would never have caught the gain in the first place. With the stock trading at $119 I can always buy it back or can wait until it takes out $200 (its all-time high).

Setting Boundaries

We all need boundaries. They are the limits that you set for what you will and won't do, and what you will and won't accept in your life. Boundaries are like invisible fences that help you deal with matters of life such as raising your kids, dealing with your relationships, keeping yourself from burning out at work, and generally staying safe in the world. We should set boundaries to manage the quality of our lives. You also have to establish boundaries when buying and selling stocks. They should provide you with starting and stopping points that alert you about when to get on and when to get off a trend.

You need boundaries to limit the universe of ideas you are even going to consider. I want to keep that universe simple so I can spend my life doing things other than a lot of research while also improving my chances of catching a trend. If a stock shows up on the list of all-time highs, I'll consider it. If I have a good experience with the company's product or service, I'll consider it. My hope is that they both coincide. I will explore whether a catalyst really exists. Other than that, I am not interested. If you stick to those two sources of information, you won't have to go searching for the next great trend. It will find you.

Boundaries versus Rules

Rules suck because they make you feel bad when you break them, but it is okay to stretch boundaries. I might have stretched my boundaries and bought Apple around twelve dollars instead of waiting for it to triple and more than confirm my belief. If you practice discipline, you can stretch your entry boundaries for ideas in which you have strong conviction.

I also stretched my boundaries to buy Chipotle when I heard they were doing an IPO. I was going to be out of town, but I put in an order to buy the stock at the market price. The price was much higher than I expected it to be. I was very upset with myself because I never expected to pay that price. I had been so confident after eating there all that time, and seeing how they ran that store, seeing how four people could run an operation like that, and how simple the menu was, and the management told me how well they were doing. Chipotle turned out to be a great stock. The point is to make your decisions easier and to force you to make a really careful, conscious decision before you stretch them. It also helps to have a strong market. Buying the best stocks in bad markets is like swimming upstream—extra risk.

There is a second reason why my search for trends relies on a list of all-time highs. When a stock hits an all-time high, everybody who has held that stock has made a profit and the last person to buy is at the break-even point. The psychology around the stock changes when it reaches an all-time high; there is a new ownership attitude because all of the people who want to sell in order to break even have sold. Furthermore, every person who has sold short (betting against the stock) is now at a loss. Those betting against the stock are losing more and more money with each tick upward. Their psychology adds upside buying fuel to an all-time high.

I think of the list of all-time highs as a database of potential big winners. When I check the new highs, I immediately eliminate ones about which I have no understanding or that I can't relate to. For example, I might find that oil is doing well, but I don't understand what all those oil companies do. It just is not in my knowledge base. I don't understand the intricacies of who drills, and who ships, and what is involved in pipelines.

Theoretically, from what I have outlined so far, every stock on a list of all-time highs is okay, but unless you have lots of money, a computer brain, and the ability to manage hundreds of positions, you have to cherry-pick. As I scan a list of all-time highs, eliminating those I don't understand or these from industries I have little faith in, I also take note of companies that I can relate to in some way. I have then narrowed down the stocks that have hit all-time highs to the few I've encountered and can understand, or maybe my sister or my kids use the product. Now those companies are planted in my consciousness.

Smith & Wesson

Smith & Wesson showed up on the all-time high list in August 2006. It was a leading brand name I could understand and one that interested me. I don't know much about guns and artillery, but I knew that Smith & Wesson was an old and established brand. When I looked at the price I thought, *Wow, that's attractive.* The stock had been going sideways for years, and now had peaked into new territory it had never been in before. So it was in uncharted waters. I love a stock in uncharted waters, and the longer it has been in charted waters, when it finally moves to uncharted waters, the stronger it has broken out. Lots of positive things can happen when a stock breaks out from a very long base.

I bought shares of Smith & Wesson in June of 2006 and was very bullish on my blog. It tripled over the next year. I don't expect lightning to strike every time I check a list of all-time highs, but it does happen. I was selling the stock all the way up because it was not a company I wanted to follow. I was willing to part with the stock and give up further gains because I had little context for it. This turned out to be the right thing to do, as Smith & Wesson cratered. Sometimes you get lucky and find them, ride them, and get off just in time.

When I experience good things or hear a lot of positive chatter about a particular product or company, it is almost guaranteed that if I look at the new all-time-high list, I am going to see that company on the list. Spend five minutes a day with Wallstrip.com or with *Investor's Business Daily* (investors.com), checking stocks that are hitting all-time highs. Look for new names on the list. For the best investment results, wait for a growing list of names.

Being Too Early

While paying attention to my experience and my experience with a product are important to me, price is the most important part in catching a trend. If you catch it too early, you could miss a lot of other things that are going on. If you catch it too late, the rest of the world may be on their way to something else as you arrive.

I was too early on Federal Express. In 1998 and 1999, I believed shipping would catch fire. Oil was a mere ten dollars a barrel. I was convinced the Internet was not a fad. Wall Street was in love with Amazon, eBay, Yahoo, and shopping on the Web, so I assumed that the shipping companies would become the most important companies of the Web. I had a "eureka moment." I felt like a genius. This was before I set my boundaries about all-time highs. It turned out that I was right, but it didn't matter, because the money was flowing into Amazon, eBay, Yahoo, and the brands that sold the products. Although it made sense that FedEx, Airborne, and UPS would be big beneficiaries of Internet shopping, none were near an all-time high. Although I was right, I was wasting time, energy, and money by fighting price. I didn't have enough money—and neither does the average investor—to be early.

I was stubborn, so my money was tied up in shipping. It was bugging me and I was getting mad at Amazon, the stock, and all the people who were in love with it, thinking, *They'll never make money, but FedEx has to ship all these books*. I was not thinking clearly. I wasted over two years of opportunity trying to prove I was right. In a sense, I was right to be big-game hunting, but it is much better to hunt where the big game are roaming.

A few years later all the Internet retailers were struggling, their stock prices were going straight down, oil prices were rising, and the prices of shipping and other logistics companies began to defy gravity on the upside. You would have found those stocks trading at all-time highs, and you would have said, "Eureka! Now I get it. My story is right. That is where the money is now flowing. Now I'll ride the trend."

In the stock market there are some bragging rights but not much else for being early. Save your bravery for the real battlefield. Don't let stocks and the stock market become your way of proving how smart you are—to yourself or your friends. Park your ego somewhere where it won't cost you anything. It also doesn't matter that you care about something. It only matters if the masses and the institutional money managers care, and that is reflected in the price of the stock. Smart and the stock market are not intertwined. The less attached you are to being right about a product or service, the more serenity you will have, and the better your judgment will become.

Being Late Sucks

By September of 2007, it was too late for Crocs. I remember Bill Maher was doing his "New Rules" bit at the end of his cable TV show. He flashed a picture of Crocs on the screen and talked about how Americans had become so fat, lazy, and casual that they had resorted to wearing plastic on their feet in silly shoe colors like orange and turquoise. At the time, I continued to love my Crocs and still saw Crocs as an incredibly comfortable product. But Bill and I were looking at it from two different perspectives. Maher and his writers knew there was a large enough audience of actual Crocs customers, so the joke would resonate. The joke was on investors.

Crocs was an old story; the jig was up. CROX at fifty-nine dollars is not the same as CROX at fourteen, twenty-four, or thirty dollars. It may be a phenomenal company and an immensely popular product that you love, but price is the final arbiter. Even though you might have just bought your first pair, it wasn't the beginning of a trend anymore. You are trying to find stocks at an all-time high, but be wary of stocks that have run 700 or 800 percent from their first all-time high.

Finding the Next Winners: The IPO Market

Ninety-nine percent of all great trends start at an IPO. Microsoft, IBM, Google, Starbucks, Ford, and General Electric all had their first day of trading. An IPO is the first clear public signal that there is something interesting going on with the company. It tells you what bankers, venture capitalists, and entrepreneurs have created.

When you are looking at companies going public, you can be guaranteed that they will be in industries that are in the public consciousness because bankers have to feel confident that they can sell the stock. In 2001 and 2002, after the Internet crash, there were very few dot-coms going public, but those that did get public had good business models. You can find hidden gems on the IPO list. If a company is good enough to get public and they need capital, they don't care about market conditions. They need the money. That IPO may struggle in the beginning. Google, for example, became public at a time when nobody thought Internet stocks could do well. Back then, homebuilders were going public and gold-mining stocks were in favor because there was a huge demand for them. The IPO market works just like any other market. It is a supply-and-demand dynamic, and you have to stay in tune with what is in supply and what is in demand.

A stock is at an all-time high on the day it comes public, but there is no context for how it has been or could be. For those reasons I will let a company age for six months after the IPO in order to get some feel for it. Do people want it or do people want out? Google came public at eighty-five dollars in August 2004, quickly went to one hundred, and was considered overvalued by everybody from the *Washington Post* to the *Wall Street Journal*. If you had waited six months you still would have fared mighty well.

I did stretch my six-month boundary for Chipotle. I put an order in the day before the IPO. I had to own it the day it came public because I really believed in the company and thought I understood the context and the story. The context was that the company would now have money to open hundreds more stores. I paid more than I expected. Chipotle was one of those one-in-a-million businesses that I wanted to own, and with that came the extra risks of chasing the IPO.

I also loved Lululemon (NASD: LULU), which came public in 2007. Lululemon is a yoga apparel chain founded in Canada. I did not chase the stock on their IPO day because, unlike Chipotle, I didn't have enough experience with their products. I wore and loved their products, but I didn't have a feel for how well their stores could do and which markets they could exploit. I was not confident in the total opportunity. Lululemon went straight up to sixty dollars but quickly back to thirty. I now have context for owning the stock if it ever did hit another all-time high.

When Chipotle came public, it already had the funding it needed and the partner it needed—McDonald's—and it had already been successful at over a hundred stores. There are blogs about restaurants that I could go to for insights and information, but a restaurant is generally a feel and an experience for me, and so something I know about because I eat out all the time.

That's why you should check the IPO list. You can find that at *Investor's Business Daily* and at ipohome.com. Those two sites give you a list of companies that are coming public or have filed to go public. This provides information about the early winners and losers and, therefore, they are good places to stay on top of new trends.

In a bad market, you will not see many companies go public because, in a bad market, nobody wants to own stock. On the other hand, if you see a lot of software companies coming public, or restaurants coming public, that is an indication that bankers are confident that people want those kinds of stocks. If you see lots of IPOs, that is usually a good time to get in the market because it is willing to take in an extra supply of stock. As always, context is important. In late 2000, there were hundreds of IPOs a week, so it is not an absolute thing, rather one of many indicators you should use to gauge the market's health.

To-Do List

1. Study the all-time-high list.

2. Wait for healthy markets for healthiest returns.

3. Don't rush—investing is about *opportunities.* Stay in the game!

4. Price trumps personal opinion.

5. There's no reason to be early and call bottoms.

6. Go with the money flow.

7. IPOs are a great place to track future winners: www.investors.com and www.ipohome.com.

CHAPTER 4

Doing Your Homework

The further you stray from stocks and businesses you understand, the more likely you are gambling rather than investing.

—RALPH WANGER, *A Zebra in Lion Country*

Homework is such a negative word. We hated homework in school from day one. I mean, who really wants to come home from their day job to work on stock research? Furthermore, what edge is a little homework going to give you over people who do this full time?

The real work is in cutting losers and in riding winners. Remember, if you are not committed to developing investment discipline, all the homework in the world will not give you an edge. You will have your winners, but your losers will absolutely crush you. Once you commit to a strategy that fits your risk profile, the most important thing you can do is use the Web and basic Web tools to pull information—and then organize that information in a way that gives you what you need with the least amount of daily effort.

Failure Happens—But Write-offs Are Overrated

I love investing and want a long career. I also like to swing the bat all the time. I don't know about hitting home runs—likely from the scrawny arm genes I carry in the Lindzon family—but I sure do try to keep hitting them out of the park. And, like most home-run hitters, I know firsthand about striking out.

As the credit crunch intensified in 2008, the total breakdown of homework (due diligence) by investors, bankers, banks, and other lenders came home to roost. Millions of Americans experienced real failure from real estate transactions. When it comes to dealing with failure, I figure we can cry about it or we can get up and dust ourselves off.

America is amazing at standing back up, but painful memories stay with us. It is the main reason why new bull markets emerge in *different* industries than previous ones. I have failed many times, none more painful or glaring as my investment in SkyNet in 1998. During the NASDAQ bubble, when we all thought we were smart, I wanted to be a shipping magnate. I was an early investor in SkyNet, whose goal was to build a global, logistic network. It was a good idea, but what the hell did I know about shipping, logistics, and global finance? The head office was in Amsterdam, so good times were had, but write-offs are over-rated!

The sad thing is that I almost pulled it off. I remember the stock going from twelve cents to eight dollars in 1999. I had not sold a share. The roll-up was cruising along. The Internet was going to make me rich! I was golfing with my buddy Tom at St. Andrews in Scotland, celebrating with money I did not yet have, when news hit the tape that SkyNet had hired a senior executive from Federal Express to take us to the next level. As I was high-fiving, golfing amid the sheep, hail, and cigar smoke, the stock top ticked. Our new CEO took us to the next level—which was *zero*—and *fast*.

This harsh lesson taught me that one must stay within one's means—because life-changing and confidence-shaking losses can happen.

Catalysts: Piecing Together the Puzzle

At the risk of overdoing a good thing and also outing myself as a total *Seinfeld* fanatic, I want to use one more classic scene from the show to illustrate a point. In this episode, Jerry and Elaine are standing at a car rental counter and the woman behind the counter tells Jerry, "We have no mid-size cars available at the moment."

Jerry replies, "I don't understand. I made a reservation. Do you have my reservation?"

"Yes we do," she says. "Unfortunately, we ran out of cars."

Stunned, Jerry tells her, "But the reservation keeps the car here. That's why you have the reservation."

"I know why we have reservations," she replies.

Jerry's retort makes the point. "I don't think you do," he says. "If you did, I'd have a car. See, you know how to take the reservation. You just don't know how to hold the reservation. And that's really the most important part of the reservation—the holding. Anybody can just take them."

Conviction *and* Discipline

The same applies to investing in stocks. Anybody can buy a stock, but you also have to hold the stock while it rises in order to make money. It takes confidence in your own judgment and discipline—your understanding about the company and its catalysts—in order to ride the ups and downs of a stock's price as a trend plays out. Trend following is not for the faint of heart. My research and understanding about a company and the catalysts for growth give me the confidence to "hold the reservation."

Conviction without discipline is a recipe for disaster. You must always have a plan and see your exit. You must have the discipline to honor your exits so that you will have the same conviction on your next go-around.

In order to complete my research, I piece together information from the Web at financial information sites, at social networking sites and other sites where I can gauge people's involvement with products, and through a network of investors who think out loud on-line and whose opinions I trust.

It is important to find businesses with strong catalysts for growth. The companies are already public so they can't be undiscovered, but they can be misvalued. The market is underestimating or overestimating the potential catalysts. To catch the big winners you must be able to gauge the company's total opportunity, the management's ability to execute at a minimum level, and where the company or product is in its life cycle. To help me understand the opportunities, I rely on these four sources of information (besides the price itself):

1. My own experience—am I excited, disappointed, indifferent?
2. On-line financial information Web sites
3. Social networking and other Web sites where I can gauge people's involvement with products

4. A network of investors who think out loud on-line and
   whose opinions I trust.

I will delve deeper into these four sources later in the chapter.
But first, below are two more examples to further explain the
full process of how stocks end up in my portfolio. Their endings
are not yet determined, but by the time you read this, the trends
could be over. I don't intend them to be predictive; I offer them as
examples of what goes into my research, and how an investment
thesis focused on a catalyst, an opportunity, a company's ability
to execute, and its life cycle all work together to help me ride out
the daily noise. After I relate these stories, I will show you where
to go to find the important elements.

Apple

The iPod was the first catalyst for the incredible run that Apple
had beginning early in 2005, when its stock rose from around
thirty dollars to two hundred in just three years. During that run,
Apple's success became less and less about the iPod and more and
more about the iPhone and their stores. Apple continued to deliver at a very high level for an extended period of time. I believe
the iPhone and the Apple Stores will continue to be a catalyst
for the company and stock. The Apple Store near my office is
in a quiet, high-end area. But anytime you walk into the store,
it seemed like people had been sucked from rest of the mall into
that one store. Apple got more traffic than the Häagen-Dazs, even
on a typical 110-degree summer day in Phoenix.

I didn't care what anyone was saying on TV, or even what my
friends were telling me, or what the hot new Apple product might
be, or complaints people had about the iPod battery or iPhone.
In my judgment, Apple's catalyst for that time and for the future
was the stores. They were impressive; some had won architectural
awards. All of them offered technical help and repairs. Many of

them offered workshops and training. It was being said that getting hired to work in an Apple Store was harder than being accepted to Stanford.

Once I understand the catalyst for a stock's success, I then want to discover if the company has an opportunity in front of it. I had to ask, How many stores might Apple have in the future? There was no telling, no comparison. Other makers of computers and electronic devices didn't have their own retail stores. Best Buy as a benchmark, maybe? They had over 800 stores. But Apple was not going to sell refrigerators and dishwashers, like Best Buy. Apple was growing at its own pace, internally controlling every detail of each store opening. Best Buy was just gobbling up chains for international growth. How many Apple Stores there would be was anybody's guess, but surely there would be many more.

Apple had lots of open field in front of it—lots of opportunity. Like a running play in football, there is all this commotion with 300-pound guys banging heads. Think of the stock market like that. There is all this banging around the line of scrimmage. Then a running back gets through that line. He just busts through, and all of a sudden, if he's a good one, he's in the clear and only has to deal with a few obstacles. It is the same thing with stocks. Once they reach an all-time high, once they break through the line where the commotion is, good things can happen. A stock that has been banging up against a certain price for a long time suddenly breaks through and, as a result, it can rise very fast.

By September of 2007, Apple had 194 stores, including stores in the United Kingdom, Japan, Canada, and Rome. If they could get to 600 stores, then, theoretically, their sales would triple. Potentially, their stock price would also triple. Talk about running in an open field.

People who had sold the stock, or had not bought it thinking it too expensive, missed the big trend. Apple was quickly becoming the best retailer in the country. Maybe the best ever created. When I walked into a store, people were not playing with the iPods anymore. They were playing with the Apple computers. Kids were playing in the kids' section. The Genius Bar, Apple's reservation-only place to go for advice and technical support, was crowded.

I still owned the stock in September 2007, but not as much as I had owned six months before. It is great to catch trends early because most people won't understand why a company is doing well—the catalyst—or what the stock might do. As the stock goes on and on, as the media gets more involved, as the price appreciates, as the end gets closer, the risk becomes higher. Whenever Apple reached a higher density of stores, people would look back and ask, Well, you grew a lot last year. What have you done for me lately? This would happen at a time when the catalyst that drove an amazing run was reaching its limit and the opportunity to open more stores was shrinking.

I wasn't predicting that this one was over; not by a long shot. But because the price had gone up, and because they had opened more stores and they had executed flawlessly for several years in a row, there was an additional layer of risk involved. We were getting closer to the end game.

In late 2006 and 2007, there were lots of stocks hitting all-time highs and I wanted to try to find other opportunities. I wanted to diversify and add new names to my portfolio, and try to find new winners as well. I felt as confident as ever in my original story and so wasn't selling all of my Apple stock, but I had been a net seller of the stock in 2007.

Gold, Oil and the Weak U.S. Dollar: Not Much Homework Needed

Be warned: You can actually do *too much* homework. If you work hard enough, you can find data that will talk you out of any stock position. The commodity trend is one where thinking and working has cost you. Following price was all you needed to do. Understanding supply-and-demand issues, lobbyists, war, pipelines, digging, have been a waste of time. Staying long and shutting up have flat-out worked. Gold and oil have been home-run trends. All the commodities and hard assets have bubbled in the last five years.

LIFETIME CHARTS OF OIL AND GOLD

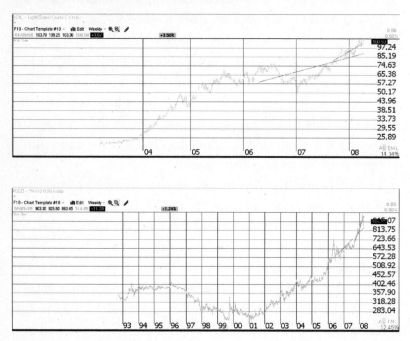

It has been such an unbelievable trend that it's hard to write about it from an unretired state. I absolutely should be retired. Insane fortunes have been made as the U.S. dollar implodes and hard assets inflate. As I write in March 2008, the price of gold is at a twenty-six-year high and oil has decisively passed one hundred dollars a barrel and new all-time highs. As a trend follower I have found this exciting, but as an investor I am curious as to how it all ends. I can't imagine a scenario where serious financial chaos is avoidable. Betting on the chaos is cool and will be sexy talk at cocktail parties, but it will most likely be unprofitable for most traders and investors.

From the end of 2001 through May 2008, oil has risen from twenty dollars a barrel past one hundred and thirty. *No* consumer good can be produced anywhere in the world without energy. The end-of-the-world bet is an exciting one, of course, but that is a homework investment. The smart investment has been to let the homework dudes fight it out and be the dumb trend follower.

From the end of 2001 to March 2008, The U.S. dollar has declined over 30 percent versus the dollar index (a basket of foreign currencies). The "talking heads" are looking for a scapegoat and generally blame Alan Greenspan along with a side of George Bush, Jr. I have my opinions and blog about them daily, but I will tell you that those focused on price love Alan Greenspan and Junior Bush.

You did not need to be early on gold and oil. They have accelerated the upward pace in 2008. *You did not need to catch oil at twenty dollars and gold at three hundred back in 2003.* In early 2006, after the trends had long been in place and oil and metal stocks were the rage, I penned "Oh, Canada":

Canada is the place if you believe in Oil, Gas and Metals. If you believe, as Richard Rainwater does, in $100 plus oil and $800 gold, why not use Canadian dollars to buy those stocks. Or, just buy some Canadian bonds. It is a leveraged way to buy those investments, much better than playing the futures markets for leverage.

The Canadian dollar has been a huge winner the last 3 years, running from 62 cents to near 90 on the US dollar. Canadians can't believe it, they don't believe it! I like that. That means they have been buying UNHEDGED all kinds of assets in the US—forever—condos, homes, stocks, bonds. They are like deers in the headlights as their US dollar investments have declined 40–50 percent, just on the CONVERSION. That is real money.

Until US monetary policy changes, the Canadian dollar is headed HIGHER—likely past par. Canadians will bring their money home again—at the wrong time—which means not anytime soon.

Yes, the strong Canadian dollar hurts the Canadian travel industry as Americans don't get the great deal they once did, but Canadians never wanted us there in the first place and we could care less about travel, we are interested in bonds, real estate and other hard assets. If you are interested in diversifying, Canada is a rather simple way to do it.

In May of 2006, I added:

Do not ignore these trends—OIL, Gold, US Dollar, Information

The case for the disappearing US dollar is real. The case for hard assets is a good one. They are both well in motion. Even if they stop today and reverse, a cascade of effects has been set in motion.

I have touched on it over the months here by following the Gold trend and goofing on the strengthening Canadian dollar that even the Canadians cannot believe.

NO ONE WANTS US DOLLARS. Buffett does not want them, global traders do not want them.

Big media has been negligent and done a horrible job covering this story so you need to find a better source.

I judge things based simply on price. The price of an asset tells you what's going on. My instincts say our leaders have lost control. It is not in their best interests to tell you that. It is a big, sometimes bad world that has developed quickly the last 5 years financially and don't be fooled—we do not have a handle.

Hedge Funds, derivatives, easy money, huge transfer of wealth, lack of leadership—IT IS A STEW that is boiling with chefs that are not fully prepared.

In May 2008, the U.S. dollar continued its horrific slide against a basket of foreign currencies. There are many reasons for the slide, but the important point for trend followers is that there has been *no* reason to liquidate your positions. It's the same trade. It turned into one of those once-in-a-lifetime investments. Gold has gone from approximately $250 an ounce to $950 an ounce, and many metals and basic materials have had even bigger percentage gains.

The powers that control our money supply continue to print money. When you print money, when you print anything over and over, you end up reducing its value. Timing the eventual deflation and ripple effects are hard, but price will lead you to winning positions.

Fish Where the Fish Are!

If you are going to do homework, think bigger picture so that you are riding the biggest waves. Focusing on the minutiae is silly. Leave that to the analysts and their interns. Think big and think long term. Position yourself so that you are thinking clearly about the future. When you are researching a company, pay special attention to the size of the opportunity and whether its business model is frictionless, disruptive, or both. Frictionless means that they are easy to do business with. Amazon is a good example. You go to the Amazon Web site and, if you have registered, it recognizes you. You click on the products you want and they go to an electronic shopping cart. With one-click buying, the system remembers your credit card information and your shipping address, and you are done. Simple. Fast. That's frictionless. Amazon still has to ship goods, but no two human beings need to talk in order to conduct a purchase transaction. There is very little resistance in the selling process. The data they have gathered allows them to enter new businesses easier than start-ups. They leverage one business to enter others—faster and cheaper.

The opposite of Amazon is . . . airlines.

No business could suck more and have more touch points of potential pain. It's not frictionless, it's "chock full o' friction." We have *all* had a bad experience traveling and hold special places of hate in our heart for certain airlines.

You want to look for disruptive companies, those that break the rules. The best example is Google. You cannot go to a store and find a Google product. Go to an Apple Store and you don't see a Google product. Go to Best Buy: no Google product. This is the leading Internet company, and they have no shipping, no packaging, no delivery. They have the best margins since Microsoft, and that has been reflected in their booming stock price. While Microsoft had incredibly high margins for their time, Google is better. Microsoft must spend money marketing. Not Google.

When we were trying to get the Wallstrip show syndicated on YouTube, a Google company, we could not dial an 800 number and talk to the person in charge of video. But they knew how to find us. One day, somehow, Wallstrip bubbled up at Google HQ somewhere and somebody tapped somebody else on the shoulder, who then tapped somebody else on the shoulder and said, "Something's going on at Wallstrip. Call them." And when you get the call from Google, you take that call. Google turned things inside out: You can't call them, but they know you. They've broken the rules.

Finance Pages

This is important. All of the information that I used to piece together my stories about Apple, Chipotle, and Crocs can be found free on the Internet. Knowing where to find that information can provide any investor with an important edge.

Google and Yahoo both have finance pages—www.finance.google.com and www.finance.yahoo.com. My main portfolio and stock-idea tracking site is www.mytrade.com. I was a founding investor in the company, and it was purchased in late 2007 by Investools (NASD: SWIM). At mytrade.com you can follow hundreds of stock investors and build your financial and stock start page. After you build it, each time you log on you will get a snapshot of the financial world and your portfolio as well as the ability to track all-time highs. You can build hundreds of stock lists.

I use Google Finance as well, where there is a Web page dedicated to every stock: a page for Crocs and one for Chipotle, for example. Those pages show charts that give a picture of the stock's performance over different periods of time—ten years, one year, and so forth. Each page also contains links to the latest news about the company, and shows the stock prices for other similar companies. For example, the page for Chipotle showed how Rubio's, Wendy's, and other restaurant chains were doing, and gave links to more information about those companies. That is how I found out how many restaurants each competitor had, which gave me a sense of Chipotle's opportunity. There are also discussion groups where investors talk to one another about the company, and links that take me to information about who owns the stock, and who is buying or selling it. These pages are invaluable resources.

People Thinking Out Loud On-Line

I also get important information and much food for thought by reading the blogs of other investors and experts in various fields. A blog is a Web site in which the blog's owner publishes a kind of journal that might include personal experiences, thoughts, opinions, or commentary about any number of subjects. Many bloggers write about their specialty. I, of course, read the blogs of people who write about stocks and venture capital.

The blogging world has its fair share of lunatics—myself included, I guess. But I am always in search of great thinkers and investors who have experience and are willing to share. I read the blogs of certain people whom I trust. You cannot put a value on that—a global community of trusted friends. I use my community in two ways:

First, if I am interested in a particular industry where I don't have expertise, I keep checking in on the leading thinkers in that industry and read about the products they use and discuss, and the products they are investing their time and money in. For technology, I read www.techmeme.com, where I get a feel for the consciousness of the technology and Web world, and for the hot buttons of the day. The goal is a quick scan of technology and Web headlines, and I see what those people believe to be important. I see what the buzz is about, and what the complaints are, and what people are excited about.

Second, I want advice from people who have been successful and from people with diverse backgrounds. When those people blog they are thinking out loud. They are not looking at blogging as if they want to teach you; they are merely using their blog as a way to think. Therefore, you have a free look into their minds. There are two key people I read in the venture capital world: Fred Wilson and Brad Feld. Wilson has been a venture capitalist for almost twenty years, and is one of the most popular new media bloggers. He blogs about life in New York and about early trends in the Internet, and his Internet investing track record is second to none. His venture funds have invested in GeoCities (sold to Yahoo), TheStreet.com (NASD: TSCM), MercadoLibre (NASD: MELI), the eBay of Latin America, Etsy.com, the on-line marketplace for all things handmade and dozens more. Daily he posts thoughts about companies he's looking at and technologies he feels are important. Brad Feld is also a very successful venture capitalist. He thinks out loud about technology and the Web from Boulder, Colorado, and Homer, Alaska. There are also technology and Web blogging generalists like Michael Parekh and Amit Agarwal (blogging from India), whom I read daily. Michael was a head Internet analyst with Goldman Sachs in the 1990s. All my favorite reads are on the blogroll at my blog, www.howardlind zon.com, and are organized in an easy-to-find way.

When you are getting a peek into someone else's mind, remember that they have biases just like everybody else. They take in huge amounts of information themselves, which can be a shortcut for readers, but you must know *how* to read them. Either way, I believe it is always valuable to glean ideas from venture capital, Web, and technology early adopters (experts) who have had tremendous success. They have the gift of being able to spot trends a lot sooner than anybody else. They can make you money. I enjoy reading the people I have mentioned and others. It is both useful and nice to find people who stretch your knowledge base, but as you become more confident with this way of investing, you will probably read less and less. If you know what fits you, you will not need anybody to tell you. Find people who are giving you ideas from a good set of data.

Control the Flow of Information

Exploring and discovery are two of the most powerful aspects of the Internet. But the Internet can also be overwhelming. You have the ultimate power to choose your information sources. I suggest you use a feed reader, sometimes called an "aggregator," to check for updates to Web sites and blogs that you determine worthy. Using a feed reader, you can create your own personal newspaper. They provide a great way to sift through hundreds of good blog authors to see if they are talking about something that is important to you. If you want to focus on stocks, you can have the blog posts of financial bloggers delivered to you through a feed reader. It is a great way to track information and it is efficient.

I use Google Reader as my feed reader. Just search for "Google Reader," sign up to use it, and start adding the blogs or Web sites of people whose writing you want to follow. Check back with your Google Reader as often as you like, and you will find what those people have written since the last time you checked. The feed reader collects them all for you so that you do not have to go searching for each of them separately, and a good feed reader will let you look just at the headlines of the articles it has collected, so you don't have to read the whole article unless the headline grabs your interest. Bloglines and Newsgator.com are other popular feed aggregators.

Does Valuation Matter?

When you are searching for information about a company, you will find a lot of talk and arguments about whether a stock is overvalued or undervalued, sometimes using the terms *expensive* and *cheap*. That is probably the most talked about aspect of investing because it's debatable. You can turn the TV to business news anytime and hear talk about a stock being overvalued or undervalued. It is the same game that is played on sports channels. Is this team good or is it bad? Are they going to win or are they going to lose? Did the team overpay for this or that pitcher? It makes sense that this happens because it fills time. What the hell else can you talk about? *Overvalued, undervalued, expensive*, and *cheap* are the most overused and abused terms in the stock market. They are "talking head" terms. For the most part, growth stocks couldn't care less about valuation, and the people who buy the fastest-growing companies do not focus on valuation, either.

Every industry has measures against which analysts judge the companies in that industry. Measures might be such things as cash flow, book value, return on equity, earnings, assets, and so forth. A standard measure across industries is P/E, or price-earnings ratio, which is calculated by dividing the current stock price by the earnings per share. So, for example, if Apple is selling at $160 a share and earning $4 a share, its P/E would be 40. P/E is measured incessantly, the objective being to find a company that is growing faster than other companies in its industry or in the market as a whole.

When someone says, "This stock is undervalued or overvalued," by whatever measure they are using, you must check the price. The "P" in P/E is very important. The price is what matters, within the context of where you think a company can grow. Stocks that are trending up will always be overvalued. They will always be considered "expensive." In both good markets and bad, there is only a limited supply of good companies. That is just the way it is. It is like tickets for a Super Bowl: there is only a certain number of them. If a manager for a big investment company likes a particular stock, even if it is expensive by traditional measures, that manager will close his eyes, plug his nose, and just buy the stock. When he does that, he drives the price up.

Don't get tricked by the valuation arguments. If you use sound entries in the best growth stocks, you will be surprised how "overvalued" your winners become. Investing in stocks is still ruled by the giant sharks you are following, and if you think you found a stock the sharks like, valuation is not the best decision point. Don't get me wrong—valuation does matter, but it only matters when a company's sales slip or slow unexpectedly. Eventually, they all slip and/or slow, even Apple and Google.

It's like weighing your child on a scale at the doctor's office. If your child won't stand still on the scale, you can only speculate about how much he weighs. If the stock doesn't stand still, you can't value it, so valuations mean absolutely nothing during a stock's growth phase. That's the way it was for Google, Apple, Research In Motion, and hundreds of other leading stocks during

2007. You couldn't know what markets were emerging for their products. You couldn't know where Apple was going next to open stores. Germany, Russia, Brazil, Turkey, China, India? You might talk with someone in one department of the company, but the company is growing so fast that a person in another department just signed a multibillion-dollar deal, and the person you talked with doesn't know about that.

Valuation matters when the market's mood shifts from complacency and euphoria to doom and gloom, but timing these shifts is a fool's game. At the beginning of June 2007, Amazon was in the sixties, Google was approaching $500, and Baidu, a Chinese search engine, was around $200. All three were thought to be overvalued. You might have concluded, "Oh my God! There's nowhere to go but down." Then Amazon spiked to near-all-time highs at $100, Google climbed to $740 , and Baidu rocketed to over $400 by the fall. Overvaluation did not matter. If you are looking to find trends and ride them, valuation is simply not your most important guide. Price direction and money management matter most.

How to Use Wallstrip

Let me give you a tour of Wallstrip.com because it is a great place (I am biased, of course) to do the kind of homework that is covered in this chapter. Go to your computer, take this book along with you, and call up www.wallstrip.com.

Each day, at the top of the wider column on the Web page, you will find a three-minute Web video show about our stock or sector of the day. After you have watched the show, read what I have to say about it from a ten-thousand-foot view, from a trend view. I tell my story about each stock we preview. Just because we cover a stock does not mean that I'm recommending it, but come each day, watch the show and see if it is talking about a company that strikes a chord with you. If it doesn't resonate with you, come back the next day and the next. Keep checking in.

The show is intended to be a snapshot of a trending business, sector, or country. We examine the business catalyst. Sometimes you will see shows about companies you are familiar with, but most of the companies will be new to you. I like to interact with other people about the stock of the day, so comments from readers are invited, and you will find a link that takes you to all of those comments.

If the company piques your interest, type the name of the company or the company's stock symbol into a Google or Yahoo search bar to find out what the company does and how the stock has done in the past. Then you can click your way to the company's Web site to find out what industries it is in, who the management is, and how the company operates.

In the narrower column at Wallstrip.com you will find all kinds of useful goodies, such as:

- A list of the top-performing companies that have already been covered at Wallstrip.com that gives you quick access to information about our winners.
- A search bar that allows you to easily browse the Wallstrip.com archives to find everything that has been written at the site about any of the companies that we have profiled. Search through the archives to see what other companies we've covered and see if anything rings true with you.
- The current list of all-time highs includes links to more information about each company.
- Links to the Web sites or blogs of other people whose opinions I trust give you immediate access to their thinking.
- You can also subscribe to Wallstrip.com or have it delivered to you by your feed reader wherever you are and whenever it is updated.

Money *spent* by the consumers and money *flow* from the in-stitutions is all you need to follow to beat the market. Combine this with money management (the real holy grail) and you will manage billions. On my blog, as in my financial life, I stick to my main money-management principles: Sell when you can, Don't be a pig, and Booking profits and paying taxes is fine. This is definitely not perfect, but it has produced some huge winners and helped me blog responsibly for three years now on the subject of trends. Start with an all-time high, take our one-a-day video blog show at Wallstrip, and digest it. If it is not for you, come back tomorrow to find out if there are any companies you should be considering for investment.

To-Do List

1. No matter how much homework you do, failure happens!

2. Price of a stock matters most. If it's not at or near an all-time high, pass.

3. Conviction and discipline are *both* important. Piece together your own story about each stock that you consider, keeping in mind its catalyst, opportunity, ability to execute, and where it is in its life cycle.

4. Find the pieces of your story, for free, on the Internet at financial pages, blogs, and other Web sites.

5. Use a feed reader like Google's to pull information to you.

6. Check in at Wallstrip.com daily for investment ideas.

CHAPTER 5

Money Management

The singular feature of the great crash of 1929 was that the worst continued to worsen. What looked one day like the end proved on the next day to have been only the beginning. Nothing could have been more ingeniously designed to maximize the suffering, and also to ensure that as few as possible escaped the common misfortune. The fortunate speculator who had funds to answer the first margin call presently got another and equally urgent one, and if he met that there would still be another. In the end all the money he had was extracted from him and lost.

—JOHN KENNETH GALBRAITH, *The Great Crash* 1929

Selling *is* survival in the stock market. In the world of trend following, the term *money management* refers to your strategy for minimizing your risks and maximizing your gains. Financial glory is not in finding trends; it is in selling losers and riding winners. You buy a stock, hopefully one that meets the criteria I have outlined, you shut out the noise of the day-to-day flow of information, and you hang on until price takes you out. As a framework for the chapter, take a look at the two charts below. They were created by

Eric Crittenden of Blackstar Funds. The first looks at compounded
annual returns of individual stocks from 1983 to 2006:

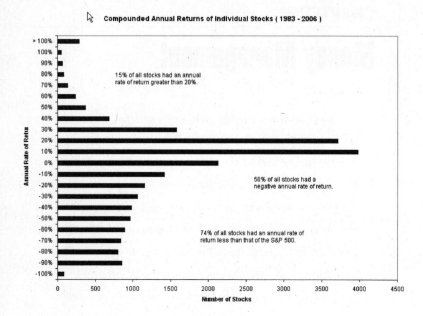

The second chart looks at delisted stocks:

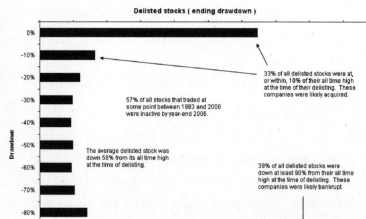

The key takeaway is that picking stock winners is extremely difficult. The likelihood of holding them makes investing more difficult, and since 33 percent end near zero, investors are really getting stuck a good percentage of the time. From the second chart you see that the strong get stronger and the weak get weaker. The money moves in and out of stocks and trends in big waves, for the most part.

Averaging Down: Dude, It's Cheaper

At the beginning of my hedge-fund and trading career, averaging down was something I heard and read everywhere. I wish I had been introduced to a mentor or trading blog that never preached the term. When you watch financial news all day, you will see mutual-fund and hedge-fund managers spew the mantra, The market is down; it's a better time to get in. I do believe there is a connection between prices dropping and stocks becoming cheaper, but stocks are just pieces of paper and who is to say what the ultimate cheap price is, or how long it will take for the rest of the world to agree with you? For the average investor, if you want to buy individual stocks, averaging down is wrong. If 33 percent of stocks head to zero, averaging down into just one in your career can be devastating—financially and mentally. Take a look at WorldCom, Enron, and, an even more recent example, Krispy Kreme Doughnuts.

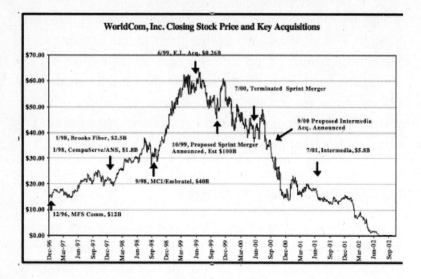

Krispy Kreme

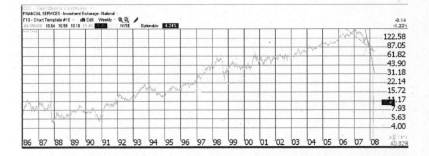

Does Timing Matter?

Focus on buying stocks at the right time—as they emerge from sideways price action. The longer the better. You can't own every stock, therefore you should concentrate on the companies and setups you feel are best. You won't get this feel overnight. You can look at hundreds of past winners, as most long-term charts look the same. You need to be like a great hitter who takes walks while waiting for his pitch. The stock market will provide you with more and more pitches for your whole life. You only need to hit a handful out of the park to make investing a profitable and enjoyable experience.

That's the good news. Here's the bad news: No matter how good your entries and how great the market is acting, many times you are going to be flat-out wrong. Whether you work at it

twenty-four hours a day or five minutes a day, there are periods
when stocks just act nasty. They fake you out and suck you in at
the precisely wrong time. The losers will come from the same list
you are looking at for winners (I delve deeper into surviving in
Chapter 6).

Your best defense is to avoid averaging down and to practice
disciplined buy tactics. Strong trending upward markets and
stocks at or near all-time highs from long bases are the best, and
if you practice, over time you will thrive. I love this quote from
Jesse Livermore in my favorite stock market book, *Reminiscences
of a Stock Operator*:

> *I did precisely the wrong thing. The cotton showed me a loss and
> I kept it. The wheat showed me a profit and I sold it out. Of
> all the speculative blunders there are few greater than trying to
> average a losing game.*

When Markets Are Good, Pounce!

After reading the first half of this book, you should be tempted
to invest money in individual stocks. But the first thing you need
to do is refrain from investing your money immediately. Instead,
look at the all-time-high lists for a month or two in order to get
accustomed to the market strength and price action. You need
context, as I said in Chapter 4. There is no rush, no need to tell
yourself, Oh, my God, I read the first four chapters and I get it.
I'm going to look at the all-time-high list tomorrow and pick ten
stocks. Wrong.

You will get a feel for the list within a couple of weeks. Then
watch it for two more weeks just to be sure. Then try to find
some companies you relate to. If there are hundreds of companies
showing up on the all-time-high list, it is likely a good time to
invest. If there are only ten or twenty, and that seems to be per-
sisting, there is no rush. It means that the market sucks, at least

for us trend followers. The reason you have to watch the list for at least a little while is to put the all-time-high list into some sort of context. Is it expanding? Declining? The more stocks you see at all-time highs, the better feel you will get for the strength of the market. That context is critical.

Take a refresher look at the long-term chart of the S&P the next time you are worried that the market will not go higher or that you feel you have to buy stocks tomorrow or you will miss the proverbial boat. Do less, watch more, and wait for great markets. When hundreds, or even thousands, of stocks are hitting all-time highs, you will make more money than you can imagine by simply riding positive trends.

Fishermen sit all day, and sometimes for weeks, waiting for the chance to reel in the big lunker. I like fishing and want to catch fish, but I am not in the business of chumming. Sure, if I go fishing for an afternoon I want to catch fish, and I even get the urge to chum, but trust me, patience pays off. You will have plenty of investing years.

Let's say that the time comes when you say to yourself: You know what? This market has hundreds of stocks breaking to all-time highs. I'm going to own stocks. If you're going to do that, try to stick to ten or twenty stocks you have a real-world connection with. Stick to stocks whose prices have been going sideways the longest and are now just hitting all-time highs. If you want to buy a stock that has been going straight up for two years, understand that it is a different risk than a stock that is just breaking out of going sideways. Stocks that have risen for longer periods of time with little sideways action are prone to rapid and deep bouts of selling.

The next thing you need to do is place an order. The hard part at this point is deciding how much money you want to invest. You need a complete game plan: what's the total portfolio size to invest, how many stocks, how much risk to take. If you want to invest ten thousand dollars and you want to follow twenty stocks, that would be five hundred dollars per stock. Think also about the commissions you will pay. Then you have to decide if you want to ease into it or just plunge in. I don't think that matters. If you have been patient and the market is strong and your setup is strong, you can plunge. If you decide to buy, what next?

Commissions

Most individual-investor portfolios need only a simple stock account. I use a company called Interactive Brokers (NASDAQ: IBKR) for my hedge fund. There are so many on-line brokerages to choose from. I have not had experience with any of the following companies, but the people from my blogroll whom I trust use:

thinkorswim—Investools (NASDAQ: SWIM)
OptionsXpress—(NASD: OXPS)
Charles Schwab—(NYSE: SCH)

You will have to find the right on-line broker who fits your needs for customer service and cost. I say take the time to learn the ins and outs of on-line brokers and the Internet so you can get the best execution at the lowest commission rates.

The Golden Rule of Trend Following or Any Investment Strategy Is Simple: Survive

Live to invest another day. There is no coming back from big blowups, and trend following has risks. Every success stems from being in the game. Anyone who cannot put that rule first needs a different book. There is no perfect way to ride a trend or to get off it, because they mean different things to different people. Riding trends and getting off them is a style and risk-management decision. I cannot possibly know such things as your financial goals and objectives or how much risk you are able to take. I do know that you can be a successful trend follower if you follow certain principles about buying and selling stocks and if you learn to spot opportunities.

If you are managing money properly, it doesn't matter what the overall market is doing. Even when the Nikkei index for the Tokyo Stock Exchange fell 65 percent between 1989 and 1992, there were certain stocks that went up, and there were ways to make money. A crash like Japan's occurred in the United States' markets after the dot-com boom in the late 1990s and early 2000s. If you were using proper money management at the time, your leading stocks were stopped out and your money would have flowed into real estate and commodity stocks as they emerged to all-time highs.

If you are managing money properly, you don't have to worry about a potential Enron in your portfolio because you will be out of any disaster like that well before it happens. Enron made greed and pop-culture news because its executives stole from the company. Unless you worked there or were not following sound money-management principles, it would not have taken you out of the investing business.

What Is Your Risk Tolerance?

Reducing your risk and maximizing your gains involves answering questions that only you can answer. Questions such as:

- How much of my money should go into stocks?
- How much of my money should go into different stock ideas?
- How much am I willing to lose on each stock?
- What is my time horizon?

There are no hard-and-fast rules. You need to set your own boundaries. Just don't lie to yourself. Investing is not a game. Assume that you will do everything wrong as an investor and ask, What is the most money I am willing to lose? The answer to this question is the total amount you should invest in stocks, and this amount should be divided by the total number of stocks you are willing to invest in and follow. It is your money, so be careful.

Here are two extreme examples. If you are twenty-five years old and serious about investing, you might decide that you want thirty years to invest. In a strong market you can be more aggressive. On the other hand, don't rely on trend following if your son is going into his senior year in high school and you are wondering how to pay his college tuition. The more time you have, the more opportunity there is for success. Less time means less opportunity.

I am in my early forties and am fortunate to have had some success. I have reliable income. I allocate a lot of my liquid or investable money in stocks because I think I have a very good grasp of what I am doing. I also am more focused on strategy and have survived many heartaches. I trust my ability to manage a certain number of stocks. At any one time I might have as much as 40 or 50 percent of that money in stocks. At the other extreme, I have rarely held less than 10 percent of my investable assets in stocks. Investors in their seventies might want a 10 or 20 percent stock allocation because they may be focused more on income than I am. A person with less experience than I have might have less money in stocks.

So my response to all of the questions above is, What can you live with? I am not going to highlight just one diversification strategy. That's because I believe that the strategy that will work best for you is the strategy you create based on the boundaries you can live with. In order to help you think about your own strategy, I will give a brief history of how my own strategy emerged and how it now works.

A Little History

In 2001, two of my friends, Cole Wilcox and Eric Crittenden, who worked for my hedge fund at that time, set out to further research investment strategies. The market had taken a serious dive and none of us was in the mood to talk about stocks. They did a lot of research, trying to discover different ways to look at entries, exits, trades, and just about everything else. We were all looking for a profitable way to manage money, and we all became enamored with trend following.

Cole and Eric began the long process of applying the trend-following systems of successful managed-futures managers to stocks. Their research, completed in 2005 (www.blackstarfunds.com), looked back at twenty-four thousand stocks over twenty-two years to test a trend-following formula. That formula involved buying a stock at the opening price on the day after it hit an all-time high, and then selling it at a ten-unit average true range (ATR) trailing stop. A trailing stop is an order to sell a stock at a price determined by a mathematical formula that adjusts the selling price in order to allow profits to run while limiting losses (the details of setting an ATR training stop are explained later in this chapter). Cole and Eric concluded that "buying stocks at new all-time highs and exiting them after they've fallen below a 10 ATR trailing stop would have yielded a significant return on average." Armed with this research, they were comfortable answering the question, Does trend following work on stocks? with, The evidence strongly suggests that it does.

Blackstar Fund, launched by Cole and Eric, is based on their research. I was an early believer, putting some money where my mouth was and becoming an early limited partner. I got an inside look at what they were building, how they managed positions, and how they built systems. It all made intuitive sense to me, and I started blogging and talking about trend following. What is in motion tends to stay in motion, in either direction. I learned that a signal to buy is a signal to buy. They look the same in every market.

Sell Is Not a Dirty Word

With the stocks you buy, you will be looking for long-term gains, not short-term gains. On the way to long-term gains, there will be a lot of losses. Using Blackstar's strategy, there would have been more that eighteen thousand trades during the twenty-two years they examined. Forty-nine percent of those trades would have been profitable. That might not seem impressive at first glance, but the use of trailing stop-loss orders would have limited losses while letting profits run, resulting in significantly larger gains for the winners than losses for the losers.

So you can make money being right 49 percent of the time if you have the ability to stop small losses from become big losses. If you cannot take those small losses time and time again, then trend following—and most likely the stock market—is not for you. If you cannot sell a stock because you are too attached to it or you are convinced it will turn around and come back to profitability, then the one time you are wrong you could have an Enron on your hands. That kind of loss can do a lot of financial damage, and it is very hard to come back from a major investment disaster.

From the moment you buy a stock, you have to be committed to selling it. Selling is the most important part of money management, and it's the place where people most often slip up. You must trust in a system like Blackstar's or you have to set some very good boundaries for yourself. Exits are essential to any trend strategy. You set boundaries for buying—stick to all-time highs and stocks and companies with catalysts—now you have to set boundaries for selling. Decide at the beginning, when you buy, This is how much I'm willing to lose on that stock. That takes a lot of the mystery and anxiety out of selling because you have a plan.

Sell When You Can, Not When You Have To

Remember this: All stock trends end. All of them. Some on their own, some because of bad management, and some sooner than most because of competition, technology, or an unforeseeable change in market conditions. If the company does not screw it up, Wall Street will. Eventually, as I have written earlier, they will create enough stock to satisfy demand and more. That supply always comes back to haunt companies, and it usually occurs as they slow.

So little time is spent on money management and even less on selling as a part of it. Selling is part art, part luck, and part discipline, but of the three, discipline is most important. Why is selling so important and, more importantly, why is it so hard?

When you buy a stock, consider it a privilege, not a right. You are in control until you push the Buy button. After you push Buy, the markets are in control. Your only remaining control is the Sell button. Of course you can buy more, but if you do your work right, you should be buying more only at higher prices. Just as there is no perfect strategy for minimizing your losses, there is also none for maximizing your gains. I use a very simple strategy: If a stock rises a quick 30 or 40 percent, or sometimes even 20 percent, I start selling. I tell myself, A profit is a profit. Take it. I want that positive enforcement. I have thought about taxes long ago, when I decided to be a trend follower. Each buy is made with the goal of it being a long-term capital gain, but if it moves quickly I am not afraid of paying taxes on a short-term gain.

Get used to taking profits by selling pieces of your winners and constantly readjusting how much money you are willing to lose. Blackstar and other systematic traders would argue that this is a science, and I would agree with them if you are investing money professionally. But if you want to do this for yourself, it becomes more a question of your own boundaries. The key is to ride the trend, and you ride it by selling on the way up and giving it a wider and wider berth to really perform longer term. The best way to ride a trend is to have sold enough on the way up that you can feel comfortable knowing it might be really wild for the next five years and you can give it the room to be wild.

Trending stocks are generally more volatile. They are in the news more and as the trend persists, as they get followed and are owned by more institutions. You will learn to give certain stocks the wider berth they need. They are like kids; you have to give them room to grow and room to make mistakes. You might also learn to tell yourself, You know what? I have a $10,000 portfolio. I think I only want to put $300 in Google, because it's wilder than the rest.

You do not have to check in on your stocks once a day, or even every other day. You should be aware of when your companies are reporting their earnings. That is not a lot of work. Use Internet tools to have the information you want to see delivered to your inbox, as I discussed earlier. You must be honest about your risk profile. To catch winners, the ones that make a huge difference to your portfolio returns, you can't sell all your winners when they move 20 percent in your favor. To own stocks, you will also endure losses and inconsistent returns.

Exits and Stops

I use trailing stop-loss orders, which are instructions to sell stocks when they fall to a certain price. There are different kinds of trailing stop-loss orders. Blackstar uses ATR stops, which they define in this way:

The average true range (ATR) . . . measures the daily movement of a security by calculating the greater of:

- Today's high minus today's low
- Today's high minus yesterday's close
- Yesterday's close minus today's low

The ATR illustrates the maximum distance the security's price traveled between the close of one business day to the close of the next business day, capturing overnight gaps and intraday price swings. There are free computer programs on-line that will help you find the ATR of any stock on any day. The ATR shows the number of cents a stock's price went up or down on average over a certain period of days. For example, on November 2, 2007, Apple's closing price was $187.87. Its ATR for the previous seven days was 4.94, meaning that the price went up or down on average $4.94 over that time. When Cole and Eric say that they employed a 10 ATR, they mean that they multiplied the ATR by ten, and then subtracted the result from the stock's price in order to arrive at their stop-order price. If you had bought one share of Apple at $187.87 on that date, and if you had followed Cole's and Eric's method, you would set your stop using this formula:

$$\text{Purchase Price} - 10\ \text{ATR} = \text{Exit Price}$$
$$187.87 - (10 \times 4.94) = 138.47$$

An ATR stop accounts for the typical movement of a stock. Every stock has its own movement. As I write this, Google moves a lot more during any particular day than General Electric, so Google needs a wider price berth than General Electric. You likely won't wake up to find General Electric down 50 percent, unless it is involved in some kind of company-killing fraud. It can happen, of course, but it isn't likely. Google, however, is a different story. It is still in the hard-to-value stage of its life cycle. Once Wall Street figures out how to evaluate it, it could go down just as fast as it went up; faster, in fact, because stocks do fall faster than they go up. You could wake up one day and see that Google's business model has changed drastically, and the stock could plunge 25 percent.

You should leave a stock like Google more room for movement. Because you have to give it more slack, you should not allocate the same dollar amount to Google as you would General Electric. Google is as inclined to fall 25 percent as General Electric is to fall 5 percent. Blackstar's mechanical trend-following method would be difficult to follow at the total portfolio level because you would have to mathematically keep track of all the positions and stops and continually adjust prices.

Another widely used trailing stop-loss order is based on percentages. Using that method, you would instruct your brokerage firm to sell a stock if it falls a certain percentage. For example, if you bought a stock at ten dollars a share and set a 10 percent trailing stop-loss order, the stock would be sold if the price falls to nine dollars. If that stock goes up to twenty dollars a share, it would then be sold if the price falls by 10 percent of twenty, which is eighteen dollars. You might want to set a higher percentage for Google than for General Electric in order to give it more room. This method is less precise than Blackstar's ATR method, but it is simpler to calculate and easier to follow.

Remember that you are creating boundaries and not hard-and-fast rules. You don't have to panic when a stock price goes down near where it will be sold, but you do have to be on full alert to decide if the catalysts and the trend are still in place. Remember also that when you start really stretching those boundaries, bad stuff starts to happen.

Picking Market Tops and Bottoms: A Fool's Game

There is a lot of sex appeal associated with picking tops and bottoms, but it is a fool's game unless you are actually in the business of doing that, like a media personality who gets paid silly money to make predictions. To be successful you will do a lot more sitting and watching. It is the news on page ten that makes big money.

Practice Your Form

If you develop good money-management habits, when markets turn bad for extended periods of time, your stock exposure will dwindle, not increase. You will automatically stay in the game. It will affect you because it affects everybody around you, but it won't be eating away at your portfolio. You will realize, I'm wrong. I'm selling. I know where to look for the next opportunities—on the all-time-high list. In the stock market, no matter what your strategy might be, you have to be disciplined.

If you are disciplined, if your form is good, if you keep doing the same right thing over and over, good things will happen. A strong market will reappear and you will have a clear mind and money to invest. Good form means that you are thinking longer term, you are sticking to the all-time-high list, and you practice sound money management. Do these things over and over and you are going to catch a three- to five-bagger. There will be periods when the ball looks as huge as a grapefruit. You can't miss. And then there will be other times when you are doing everything right and it looks like a seed. You can buy the greatest growth stock in a bad market, and the next day, after it hit an all-time high, it is down ten points. It happens.

In 2007, I caught four in a row: Apple, Chipotle, Crocs, and Baidu. I got into that sweet zone where the ball looked as big as a grapefruit. I considered myself lucky, and I did not overthink it. I did not try to pick a top, but as I blogged throughout 2007, I took profits along the way. I knew all four were overvalued in the "textbook" form of the word, but I let the price dictate my action.

The best thing that can happen for you is a good market. If you stay in the game, a good market will eventually come along, like an ocean that just sweeps you and everyone else with it. It is a beautiful thing to be swept along with the flow of money, and there will be periods of great returns. It won't always be like that. There will also be periods when owning stocks is painful to your wallet. Google won't run. Chipotle won't run, even if they're opening fifty stores a week. Few stocks will be hitting all-time highs. The mood will have changed in the market as well, and you will end up watching from the sidelines because your money management will have automatically taken you out of all that mess. You may have lost some percentage of your money, but those losses will generally have come after your biggest gains.

Cheating: Fear and Greed

This usually happens after prolonged good runs and bad runs. You cheat. You try to pick a bottom or turning point. You buy a stock early, predicting an all-time high before it happens because the market is strong. We all cheat. It is lazy and we know it, but we do it. Maybe the stock is only 5 percent away from an all-time high and the market is good. I did that with Coinstar (CSTR), the company that owns self-service coin-counting machines. I saw their machines because my wife uses them, and I became enamored with the company and started following it.

I bought the stock about 5 percent below an all-time high, on the way up. Coinstar's earnings came out and the stock fell hard. I got stopped out. I crossed a set boundary by gaming an all-time high, and I also bought the stock just before an earnings announcement. I suffered the consequences when the earnings were announced. I watched the stock fall rapidly and got stopped out. If it had gone up one more dollar to an all-time high before I bought it, would I have felt better about it? I actually would have; I would have lost more money paying out that additional dollar and end up getting stopped out anyway, but I would have avoided feeling that I'd jumped the gun and gotten a little lazy about sticking to my boundaries. What I should have done was watched it a little longer and not stretched my boundaries.

I tend to make the cheating mistake, but I have not been immune to greed and tips. It rarely ends well. Examples follow later in the book.

Financial Leverage: A Dangerous Tool

I have seen it firsthand and it is evil. Fortunes have surely been made, but leverage—borrowing to invest in the stock market—is not something I could recommend for the average investor. Not ever. I think it can be used for a day or a week, and, at the proper times, for a month or two, but only as a short-term tool. To use it as a constant strategy is just is not smart for 99 percent of investors. Leverage is a very dangerous tool because things unwind very fast in the stock market.

In 1999, I was a partner in a small broker-dealer. I was overmatched, but that's another book. One of my partners was a wealthy, wealthy man. He had made and lost fortunes in the scrap business and was in a fortune period. We had grandiose office space and were riding high. We were our biggest clients. He had leveraged his blue chip Waste Management stock that he earned from selling his scrap business to CMGI, Yahoo, Amazon, and the rest of the tech bubble. He was, for a time, *killing* it. Goldman Sachs, his lender, loved him too. I knew nothing, of course, because I would walk into his office while he was barking out 20,000 shares CMGI buy orders to tell him he should be selling. He would be up $100,000 by the time his confirm was back. I was the "putz," the "wimp."

I remember the summer of 1999, because that was the beginning of the end for my partner and our firm. Waste Management was basically halved in price on accounting "discrepancies." I love that word *discrepancy*. The real meaning: fraud! Goldman Sachs was calling, but for a different reason this time. Not to lend, but to collect. When you get a margin call, don't ignore it. Sell what you can to pay it off the minute you get it and move on. De-leverage. My partner did not. When Waste Management contin-ued to drop and the Internet stocks began to tank later that year and into 2000, it did not take long to unwind twenty years of hard work. It took six months, actually, helped by a loose Gold-man Sachs and a lack of basic money management and discipline. Combined with the eventual Waste Management liquidation to meet margin calls and the tax consequences of the sales (still a capital gain), the losses were crippling. The amount lost was well north of $50 million: real money.

In a good market, leverage works great. You buy a hot trending stock, and the money you borrowed doubles or triples, and you forget you borrowed it in the first place. Using leverage like that makes you feel giddy on the upside, but you can blow up very quickly. The only way to stay in the game and find that next great trend is not to blow up. Even if you are right about leverage and it works for you the first time, it will come back to haunt you.

Summary

Focus on the following items to make money from trend invest-ing:

1. Scanning the all-time-high lists for the best stocks you can relate to and understand
2. Narrowing your selections down to the companies with the most unique growth opportunities, and
3. Focusing on a system that allows you to ride those winners as long as possible.

To-Do List

1. Survive. Don't let one trade or investment put you out of business.

2. For every major money-management decision, ask, What losses can I live with?

3. Never buy a stock without an exit strategy.

4. Make use of trailing stops.

5. Sell on the way up.

6. Paper trade and slow down. There is no rush.

7. Financial leverage: avoid.

CHAPTER 6

Bear Markets: Reduce Mistakes and Survive

The world needs ditchdiggers, too!
—TED KNIGHT, *Caddyshack*

It is important to remember that "bear" markets happen. You need to get through them with as much capital as possible. In a bear market, what you buy, when you buy, and what you pay *matters* much more than in a bull market. If you learn how to recognize bad markets and position yourself accordingly, you will make money in the next bull phase. The great news about our position in time as investors is that it won't matter where or when the next great bull phase occurs. Financial technologies, ETFs, and the global pursuit of money will make future bull markets more profitable than ever.

The quote at the top of this chapter is fantastic; it's from one of my favorite movies. Stocks don't care whether you are rich or poor, love them or hate them, long or short. The markets will take your money. If they go down the minute you buy them, it's not their fault, the company does not suck, and you are probably not stupid. If they rocket the minute after you buy them, you are definitely not a genius. If you buy stocks at the right time, consistently, you will make money. Period.

I have tried to show you how to find the "next Starbucks" simply by studying the all-time-high list. In short, proper money management separates the winners from the losers. One thing we can do to put the odds further on our side is avoid catastrophes. That's not easy, but in the real world of investing, most investors (those not making a career in the stock market) have to be choosy. We have limited time and investment capital. We have real jobs and real financial issues, like education, health, and family obligations.

Let me give you an example. I am a 6- to 8-handicapper in golf. When I am playing well, I can shoot near par. When I am off, the 80s are more likely. I don't play golf daily, or even weekly—I play golf to relax and to network—but I still want to shoot low. That's the objective. The best way to do that is to hit fewer "bad" shots. I don't play enough to hit great golf shots consistently, so for me, it's extremely important to keep the ball in play and to manage the golf course. Take what the course gives you. People who golf with me are always shocked by my abilty to play. They remind me that I don't look athletic, my swing is crooked and short—I just get the ball in the hole. My mantra is "It's not how, it's how many!"

It's the same for the average investor. If you follow my guidelines for finding winners and then use proper money management, you are on your way.

There's No Stopping the Business Cycle

Like genetically created veggies and fruit, modern finance has tried to rid the economy of business cycles. Unfortunately, there is no ridding the populace of greed and fear. We have Prozac (for depression), Lexapro (for anxiety), Ambien (for sleeping), and Monster energy drinks, but we can't seem to do anything but prolong the inevitable cycle.

In my experience, it's the peaking of fear and greed that "tip" the cycles. In the United States, we fear the second coming of the Great Depression. That makes sense. It was horrible. Our greed comes from a misplaced confidence that our knowledge will prevent a recurrence. That sounds good on paper. But in truth, I don't think the markets care that you are fearful or greedy. As such, if you invest, expect to experience a bear market.

Take a look at this chart of the most recent bubbles (courtesy of BespokeInvest.typepad.com). Remember that after each bubble (not including China because, as of this writing, it was bent but not broke), the end of the world was predicted. If you are reading this book, that, of course, never came to pass. In any event, the first element that stands out for me, although not statistically significant using three examples, is the shrinking timeline. The railroad bubble played out over forty years. In our efforts to control bubbles, we may be creating them more quickly. I will leave the real debate up to the economists, "talking heads," and *analy*sts.

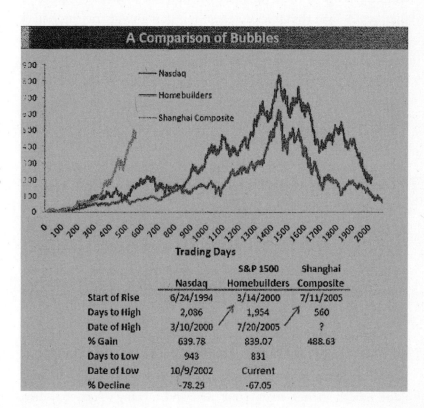

	Nasdaq	S&P 1500 Homebuilders	Shanghai Composite
Start of Rise	6/24/1994	3/14/2000	7/11/2005
Days to High	2,086	1,954	560
Date of High	3/10/2000	7/20/2005	?
% Gain	639.78	839.07	488.63
Days to Low	943	831	
Date of Low	10/9/2002	Current	
% Decline	-78.29	-67.05	

Bear Markets, Like Shit, Happen

Again, if you invest for real, you will run into bad markets. No matter what you own, it will drop and there will also be fewer stocks and ideas to choose from. I now embrace these times. They separate the skill from the luck. In bull markets we all look smart. In bear markets we feel stupid, but the disciplined get rewarded. Unloading your best stocks after they have dropped 25 to 30 percent from all-time highs is an awful feeling. It feels wrong, but in the business of trend following, it is inevitable. You must have discipline.

There is no boogey monster or plunge protection team. Even if you are a conspiracy theorist, do not let it rule your life. I never trusted George W. Bush or Dick Cheney, but I also never believed that writing bad things about them was going to get me audited. I am not paranoid. I don't let my distrust of people in government or in the market infiltrate my life and influence my investment decisions. If the government takes us to war, military stocks are going to do better; that is just common sense, and that's what matters in the market. Price will lead you.

The market is a giant ocean of flowing money and, as with any wave at the beach, you are going to get smacked in the face occasionally. If you think that is the fault of other people, you are not going to make money. In reality, the sharks are definitely out to trick you. If Goldman Sachs wants Google to be higher or IBM to be higher, and if they have to drive it down 20 percent to get it to go up higher, they can and will. You have to know your enemy, but if you start to feel pissed off and victimized, you will sell at the wrong time.

Allowing yourself to feel victimized will also take away your confidence. When in doubt, take another look at the long-term trends in U.S. markets. They show clearly that you do have a chance. If you think the boogeyman is out there and is going to get you, then look in the mirror. That boogeyman is yourself. You are your own worst enemy. If your confidence is low, then do less, invest smaller amounts, and when you feel confident again, increase the stakes a little bit. There is no need to rush unnecessarily.

You have to take responsibility. You wrote the check, or you called the broker, or you pushed the Buy button on the computer. The great news is that you can always change your mind in the stock market.

It is said that the average bull market lasts thirty-six-plus months and the average bear eighteen months. If that's the case, you will encounter a horrible market within the first three years you invest. That being said, the 1990s basically went straight up and we had to pay for our sins only after March 2000. The real estate boom that began after 1990 was an even longer cycle, basically peaking—at least for homebuilder stocks and land speculators—in 2006.

As we began 2008, a global credit and stock crisis began to unfold. The NASDAQ experienced its worst January ever. Those most prepared will be best positioned for the next leg up. Remember, in bear markets your goal is just to survive and to preserve your capital.

Following is a series of thoughts on things that go wrong and things to watch out for while protecting your capital in the next "bear market."

Recessions

All media has a field day with the word. There is a fascination with growth. Our leaders have become slaves to the economy. So, in my opinion, to believe in the word *recession* would mean you have to buy into the data that the government feeds you. That's a conflict in the United States. I just prefer to watch the markets. When stocks are dropping like flies from my portfolio, I know the markets suck and the mood of the country is terrible. If it persists, people get hurt financially and react. Productivity drops, and of course growth slows. Forget the term *recession proof*; there is *no* such thing as a bear-market-proof stock. In 2008, every leading category from China to solar to health care was ravaged. Trends just ended in clumps. Even Humana (BlueCross BlueShield), fell more than 50 percent. People obviously felt that dying was cheaper than worrying about it.

Don't Get Mad, Get Liquid

First off, we all lose in a bear market. Some just lose less. A bear market is basically a 10 percent decline in stock market averages. I wish it was that easy to define. I have been a hedge fund manager through a few vicious bear markets, and they're lousy. I liken the experience to a walk in the Dead Sea in Israel. You are warned before you take a plunge that the salt will find any slight cut in your skin and you will feel the pain. A bear market will cause any equity exposure pain. But here's the thing: New leaders will emerge from bad markets. They emerge, but usually only a few investors care and only a few believe. If you are busy buying value, managing losses, and mad at your dwindling portfolio from a bear market, you will miss out.

The best athletes generally have the best fundamentals. Tiger Woods is my favorite athlete to watch. He is so good that he can routinely get out of trouble, but when he dominates he is playing golf from the fairways, not the trees. He has learned to manage his swing and not go for 350-yard drives each and every time. It is a simple analogy but true. Tiger is patient. You should learn from him. All you need to do is wait and just stay in the game. In bad markets, you need to do less. If you keep an eye on the emerging trends, avoiding prolonged weak markets will be easy. If you can't, you should read my blog and you will be up to date.

One other important caution: You are in control until the Buy button is pressed. There is no one to cry to and no one to blame. Participating in the stock market is a privilege, but it is treated like a "right" by too many. If you are buying strength, specifically all-time highs, and doing it well, you will decrease your exposure to weakness and increase your exposure to strength. If you want to do what Warren Buffett does at Berkshire Hathaway, just pay the premium and buy his stock or that of one of his disciples. I am always amazed at how investors get mad at the stock market and stocks. You are getting mad at prices. Prices don't care and prices don't lie. If you are getting mad, you are wrong. If you are investing on leverage or you are not in a financial position to own risky assets like stocks, don't invest. Invest in yourself.

Reducing Mistakes: Avoid Tips

The tip trend has been alive since the beginning of time. This is an example of a good tip: "Don't smoke in bed!" Here's a bad tip: "My cousin-in-law Frank says . . ."

The financial world does a piss-poor job of talking about mistakes. Too bad. That's how we learn. On my blog, I try to own up to my big mistakes. And one mistake we are all guilty of making is listening to tips. It will happen to you if you have invested. If this is your first investment book, I am glad you are reading this. If you have read many investment books, let this section serve as a reminder: Receiving *tips* is going to cost you. Stop giving them as well.

Through the years, I have received many stock tips and never made a dime. My most recent tip debacle was on a company called PlanetOut.com (LGBT). The company offers products and services to the worldwide lesbian, gay, bisexual, and transgender community. It is the largest gay media Web business. I was talking one day with a really smart investor whom I trust immensely, and he walked me through the story. He likes to take big stakes in businesses that are "undervalued," so this was not a different kind of proposition for him. On paper, it sounded phenomenal. The stock had gone straight down from when it did its IPO. I bought a lot of the stock under two dollars. This is not what I normally do. I broke several of my boundaries: It wasn't at an all-time high, and I bought it based on someone else's opinion.

When I talked about having bought it on my blog, my community made fun of me. It rose to two dollars, and I sold some, so that was smart, right? I made some money, which is probably the first bad thing that happened. Then Bill Gates became the largest shareholder of the company, so now I felt like a genius. Of course it wasn't Bill Gates personally, but the people who manage his money. That news hit the wires and I said, "Okay. Cool. I beat Bill Gates to this idea." Meanwhile, Bill Gates has probably never heard of it. Then the stock drifted down again and I thought, *Well, now I'm going to buy back at the same price that I sold.* Then it just plummeted farther. After all of that I was in San Francisco with my wife and kids, and I saw the sign for the PlanetOut offices. We were walking up a hill, and I said, "Honey, that's—" and I stopped myself. I was too embarrassed to tell her I owned the stock. I was actually thinking about sneaking away from my family to go into their place and yell at them for their horrible business. I was stuck, meaning I never should have bought that stock. Then I should have picked a point to sell it all. I should have been happy to sell all of it at two dollars, and never looked back.

I didn't do any of those things. I compounded my mistakes by continuing to follow it. That is what happens when you own a company or stock and you have no idea why you bought it. There is no entry point that makes sense, and no clear exit strategy. I was a schmuck for owning the stuff in the first place. I still own a little bit of PlanetOut, and I am keeping it as a reminder of how stupid I can be. There are too many mistakes in this story to count—I made them all.

Stick to keeping it simple and doing your own work. So if you get a stock tip, say thank you and then just forget about it—unless of course they have a blog; then it's gospel.

Reduce Mistakes: Avoid Cheap Stocks

Cheap stocks are cheap for a reason. I will almost always avoid stocks under ten dollars a share, and other than the extreme stupid behavior (when I really feel like losing money—see PlanetOut example), buy stocks under five dollars. So many great investment books have covered this topic and they are just correct.

As trend followers this is even more important. Trend investing means we will never be first. Momentum stocks always get overvalued and you will find plenty to choose from in the teens, twenties, thirties, and higher. When you do, choose from the higher-priced, more liquid stocks; they will have lots of institutional support and liquidity for you to manage your positions.

Focus: Be an Expert in One Discipline

America offers us the luxury of building wealth from doing one thing well. Being a jack-of-all-trades is nice for MacGyver and getting invited to cocktail parties, but is not an important requirement for investing. The best investors stick to those products or services they know.

Brad Feld and Fred Wilson, the two venture capitalists I interviewed for this book, leave the stock market alone. Brad Feld told me that his overall success as an investor in the stock market was not as good as he would like. He said, "When I thought about my behavior, the reason that I wasn't doing better was that I am so busy doing what I do on the private side that I really wasn't paying the appropriate attention, or working with the appropriate depth, on the public side. I was behaving irrationally like so many other people do. I'd get emotional about something and sell."

Fred Wilson had a similar experience. He bought stock in biotech companies in the late 1980s. He said, "I didn't really understand biotech very well but I was fascinated by it. At the time I didn't have much money. I don't remember what stock it was that blew up first, but it just blew up. It just cratered. It went down by fifty or sixty percent." Now Fred says, "The amount of money that I invest in public stocks is trivial."

Wilson believes the business of a venture capitalist is investing in an early, private valuation and getting paid by either a take-out or a public offering. He said, "If the public offering gives me ten times my money, I take my ten times my money and I don't play for another two times or three times in the public market because I can give it back just as easily as I can get it."

Venture capitalists do not always exit after their obligations are completed. Feld was a seed investor in Critical Path, a software company. He held the stock during the period after the IPO when he was obligated to hold it. He said, "I had a strategy where I sold half of my stock, and if the stock started to come down, I sold half of whatever remained until I didn't have enough shares to care anymore and sold them out."

For the most part, venture capitalists, like you, have to stick with doing what they do well. They need to take the money that they made and reinvest in new ideas. Feld makes a distinction between what he calls seed investing and classical institutional investing. He explained, "The seed investment is when you are trying something and you are willing to lose all your money quickly and just walk away from it. The next round is when you believe that you've got something, and you are going to try to build a meaningful business out of it."

Feld's company was a seed investor in a company called PeoplePC. When PeoplePC came public in 2001, it closed on the first day at eight dollars. He said, "The company went public with 100 million shares that was worth a billion dollars for one nanosecond—the first trade. By the time we sold the company, we got 2.5 cents a share. Fortunately, it didn't go bankrupt, but we rode it all the way down to zero. The heartbreaking ones are the ones where you have hundreds of millions of dollars of gain that you rode all the way to failure. The end result is my philosophy today: my investors don't pay me to be a public company investor. They pay me to be an early-stage venture capitalist. "It's a huge lesson that I learned from the dot-com bubble," he continued. "All of a sudden I started doing investments in stuff I knew very little about. While some percentage of the skill that I had did apply, the vast majority of it didn't, and I found myself over and over losing money in the stock market. I was checking Yahoo quotes 300 times a day, following my stocks."

Expect Mistakes

There is no perfect strategy, no holy grail, no smooth investment return line to be had. Even Warren Buffett struggles. He was considered a has-been and washed up during the late 1990s tech bubble. Losses will happen. Along with all of the pitfalls I just mentioned, you are competing against the smartest people with the most money in the world. They may want a stock to be in one place, but they start out in a different place because they know that they have the money to move it to the place where they want it to be. When the market turns against you, when the train starts backing up, when you get head-faked, you have to cut your losses. When the market sucks, go do something else.

Venture capitalists are stuck with the same kinds of problems that public investors face. Some don't want to get in too early because there is no market. Some want to be investors before there is any product because they see a future. They also have the same problems you have concerning when to sell, and they make the same mistakes you make. Sometimes they should sell and don't practice good money management. They let a company go public and get greedy, saying, "This is just the beginning," but stock investing is different and the markets can treat a company much differently than a few private investors.

Also, again like you, venture capitalists have to focus on staying in the game. Failure is part of their business, too. The best of them screw up a lot less than the average. They can't sell their losers like you can sell them. They can get creative and try to raise more money, but if in their hearts they know there is not a business there after six months or a year, they are screwed. It is hard way to make a living. In the stock market, you can change your mind the next day—how great is it that? If you stay away from cheap stocks, you get liquidity as well.

When I was interviewing Fred Wilson for some insights about trends and venture capital for this book, he told me his worst investment was a company called Urban Box Office. He said, "The premise was the urban marketplace comes to the Internet. It was streetware, hip-hop, African-American culture, being delivered in a Web experience to a commerce community."

When I asked him what went wrong, he told me, "Everything. It was a bad investment premise because there is no real urban segment. Then the creative front man for the business died a month after we made the investment. Then we put another round into the business after he died. The company was mourning and was running out of money, and we put more money in and we shouldn't have."

As a venture capitalist or a trend follower, you get whacked, you have successes, over time you develop boundaries about how you are going to do things, you do what you do best, and you always have a plan for selling. Fred and the rest of the best venture capitalists have a plan for exit before they invest—just like you and I should.

Just Say No: Everlasting Pain-in-the-Ass Industries

You can't own everything, so you might as well own the best. In great markets, hundreds if not thousands of stocks will hit all-time highs. There are just certain industries and stocks you should avoid. If you are overwhelmed by all the choices and opportunities in the investment world, it may be a good idea to cross off the industries below for the reasons that follow them:

- Airlines: Unions
- Computer Hardware: Asia, Life Cycle, Margin Pressures
- Consumer Electronics: Asia, Life Cycle, Margin Pressures
- Components Companies: Those companies not in control of prices in their chain of supply. Always ends badly.

Number one on the list is airlines. Entrepreneurs and big institutional money are attracted to the space because of operating leverage. But it has rarely translated into long-term shareholder value. Remember that we are the low guys on the totem pole (common stock). I also say no to any business with unions, which includes most stocks where the government has to be involved, like drugs and biotech. I also cross off anything I don't grasp, where I don't trust my intuition. I do not trust my intuition about fixing things. Changing a lightbulb can cause me grief, for goodness' sake. Do not send me to Home Depot. I get dizzy and faint. I am also a little bit like that when it comes to information technology, especially hardware and components. Component stocks have broken my heart. They are sexy and enticing because they trend. They have vicious endings, though. Component companies can be performing phenomenally but in the end, companies that they depend upon, like Hitachi and Toshiba and Apple, may say, We love you and you are doing a fantastic job but, you know what? We're going to do something cheaper. We (common shareholders) never hear that first call. When those calls get public, component stocks crash and crash hard.

The "guts" business is sexy and lucrative, but it will break your heart. Let me give you a painful example, actually two in the same stock: Synaptics. I have let myself get burned not once, but twice, riding this stock. Synaptics was on fire during the early iPod boom as they were the suppliers of the click wheel and touch technology. Sales were booming, as was the stock. It felt like my secret because the mainstream media never talked about the stock. That did not matter because every Apple employee involved in making the iPod wanted to improve the design and cut costs so they could sell more iPods. Component companies are at the whim of all their masters. If you want to own them and ride them, sell them early and sell them often.

It's the Dollars That Count

When I asked Fred Wilson what he believed to be the biggest mistake made by both venture capitalists and investors, including those of us who follow trends, he told me, "The mistake that my peers in the venture business make is they focus on valuation and ownership at the expense of dollars invested." If Wilson wants to invest $3 million for 20 percent of a business, implying that the company is worth $12 million, and a competitor offers $5 million for 20 percent, implying that the company is worth $20 million, the entrepreneur can get seduced by the fact that the competitor is valuing the company higher. The competitor is making his exit harder.

Wilson said, "What is important in the business is the raw multiple of the money invested, so therefore I would rather turn $1 million into $20 million than $5 million into $30 million because I want to make the biggest multiple of gain." Many of Wilson's competitors think the way they do because they want to manage ever larger amounts of money. They become asset gatherers and start thinking, "How do I create a billion dollars because on a billion dollars I'm getting paid two percent on a billion dollars. Think about all that income."

Investors in stocks, trend followers or not, make the same kind of mistake. They see Google at six hundred dollars and think, *That's expensive. I can't buy two hundred shares, so I can't own that stock.* It isn't how many shares you own that counts—it is the dollar amount you pay. Don't be afraid of buying six-hundred-dollar stocks even if you can only buy a small number of shares. Don't buy three-dollar stocks because you can own more shares. Buy the best stocks, even if you can only own a few shares. The Internet has blessed us with cheap commissions to make it possible.

Manage the Fear

Fear is a normal part of any investment. There are so many things that can go wrong, even in a fantastic bull market. With trend following, the market can get very volatile, and the volatility in a venture capitalist's world is at an early stage, with a lot of unknowns and uncertainty. I asked Brad Feld about the emotional side of his world. He said, "You have to manage to get rid of all the emotion about making investments. It's not dispassion. We are enthusiastic about all the things we do, but that moment of closing the investment doesn't give you that emotional charge. That really comes from building something significant and having a great exit. The process of building something significant has lots of ups and downs. Things work, things don't work, you're happy, you're unhappy, you love the CEO, you hate the CEO, they win a big contract, a big competitor comes to their market and you get screwed for a while. Google buys a competitor and all of a sudden you fear and feel tortured. [Author's note: Yahoo buys a competitor, then you cheer because you know that that competitor's going to disappear from the face of the earth.] That is just part of what we do."

Feld was an early investor in Sling Media, which was bought by EchoStar. Their first product, the Slingbox turns any Internet-connected PC or laptop, Mac, or smart phone into your home television. That means you can watch TV virtually anywhere in the world. He continued, "The moment at which it was announced that EchoStar bought Sling for $380 million—that is the moment that you cheer."

Trend followers need to develop the same kind of dispassion that Feld describes. It is very much the same in the process of following a stock. It goes up, it goes down. You have a certain set of boundaries about entering, but the exit is what matters. Winning is about how you manage the process after the investment.

Hope Is for the Hopeless

Hope has no place in the stock market. It is okay to hope for world peace. But if you are hoping about any stock in your portfolio, that it won't go down any more or that something good will happen to it, you own the wrong stock. You may be too leveraged, as well. You must stay in charge of your money, whether you are doing it yourself or having it managed by a broker.

Keep It Simple

When you are running a strategy, any strategy, you have to stay focused on it and keep it simple.

When following trends, remind yourself often that it is about all the opportunities, about the trains leaving the station, and about getting on and getting off according to a strategy. Simple. Yes, you may have not recognized a trend when it first started, and you may have sold too early one time and too late another time. The good news is that money will move through the system all the time and you have a strategy that will work over time.

In order to keep things simple, you won't hear much from me about shorting stocks, or about investment derivatives such as futures contracts, forward contracts, options, and swaps. If you get excited about stocks and the market in general, you may get seduced by the sex appeal associated with doing it faster, asking yourself, Why not? Why shouldn't I? Won't these alternatives make things happen faster? I have tried all the derivatives and strategies, and for the average investor they are a waste of time and energy. In the right hands they may be good, but in the wrong hands they are like fire: dangerous. If you look at the Forbes 400 Richest People in America list, you don't see short sellers at the top of that list. You see Bill Gates, Warren Buffett; you see media barons. These are people who continue to be positive and invest straight-up in stocks and individual businesses. Betting against stocks is complicated and negative; you don't need to do it, so just cross it out.

An even simpler way to participate via stocks than the trend-following methods I am describing is investing in exchange traded funds (ETFs). These are baskets of related stocks that are traded on the stock exchanges. For example, you can own PowerShares Water Resources Portfolio (PHO), which is a group of water-related stocks. Owning an ETF means that you are not focused on just one company's risk and reward; you are focused instead on a group of them. An ETF gives you a better chance to capture a trend; maybe not as fast, because one company can do a lot better than a group of companies as a whole. However, if you don't understand a particular industry but you want to be involved, an ETF will give you exposure. ETFs are also a phenomenal tool to give you diversification across industries and even across countries—you can own, for example, a China ETF.

No Such Thing as a Sure Thing

John Henry, the owner of the Boston Red Sox, is a trend follower. He has no opinions. This guy sees something in motion and gets on it. He hops on that train, not knowing exactly where it will end up but knowing that it is going in the direction he wants to go: up. When you get on that train and you know it is going up, in three minutes it could reverse. That happens in the stock market. A stock goes up, shows itself to everybody, and then all of a sudden the conductor says, "You know what, piss on this—we're going back the other way." So you get off; you have to get off. Why keep going in reverse, thinking that the conductor is going to change his mind again and go up? You just have to keep going, moving forward. I would bet that John Henry thinks, *If I get on enough trains going in the right direction, I'm going to be on the one that goes just exactly where I want it to.*

Trend following is not for the faint hearted. If you want certainty, don't do this. If you want certainty, you are in danger of getting sucked in by someone selling you a supposedly foolproof system. They will charge you thousands of dollars and you will get a crappy piece of software on your computer, and the minute it stops working, you will freak out and give up.

Instead of spending your time asking, Why? spend it looking for ten other trends.

Be True to Yourself

Comfort plays a role in performance. I have a closet full of suits that cost me a lot of money. People tell me I look good in them, but I don't feel good in them. They are not my style. Why should I dress like a shark when I don't think like one? I like being the "Larry David" of money management. If you are uncomfortable buying stocks, the indexes and ETFs are fine ways to invest your money.

If what is going on inside you makes sense, what you are wearing on the outside doesn't necessarily have to, as long as it helps you think clearly. Wearing T-shirts and Crocs helps me think clearly. Sometimes you have to conform, but less so in today's world than in the past. That argument rages on and on, and I am sure that tons of money is made in the fashion industry over that debate. But Google is showing how important "conformity to the norm" is to performance: It is not. Comfort is important, though, and it's gaining importance as our culture gains more importance overseas. Google realizes that their cost is in brains and people. Therefore, they are trying to remove the everyday anxieties their employees may have. The fastest-growing company of all time feeds their employees gourmet food, and scooters lie around their offices and campuses. They have game rooms with Ping-Pong tables and pool tables, and they give their people a certain amount of time for their own work and projects. They have health care at HQ, day care for kids, and you can bring your pets to work.

Keep a Diary

You should get into the habit of building lists and keeping a paper or electronic diary. It does not have to be as involved as a public blog. At worst, it is an exercise in keeping track of the market leaders. Grab a yellow legal pad and just jot down names. This is a great exercise to get a feel for names and industries that continually show up on your lists.

You have to be aware of your strengths and weaknesses and how they affect your investments. I write my blog as a way of holding myself responsible. However you decide to do it, in a blog or a diary, write down your thoughts. Look at your account monthly or quarterly and make notes about things such as how good or bad you have felt about buying and selling, or whether other people are influencing you too much.

When you look back, notice, for example, if your thoughts have been negative. If they have, you should be doing less until you get through that phase. Or, if you have not been making money while the market as a whole has been doing well, you know you are doing something wrong. You can't lie to yourself. Also, find a trusted group of people or sources who know you well, whom you can go to in order to check on how you are doing as a person, and

To-Do List

1. Business cycles can be extended but not stopped—learn how to recognize big market trends.

2. If you invest for more than three years, at some point you will likely encounter a bear market.

3. Avoid acting on stock-market tips at all costs.

4. Jot things down, make lists of top stocks, and keep a diary of some kind. It does not have to be greatly detailed.

5. Fear is normal, but you are in control of your money. Pick a style that works. If it's cash, so be it.

CHAPTER 7

The Trend Is Your Friend

It's not where the stock has been—it's where it could go.
—Howard Lindzon (Me)

In my preference to keep it simple, I often refer to the saying: "The trend is your friend." You could also say: "If it ain't broke, don't fix it." If you are investing, much like hunting or fishing, you might as well catch big game. If your money is at risk, you might as well look for big gains.

Don't invest for specks of meat and flesh when there is real meat on the bone.

In the stock market, individual stock surprises generally happen in the direction of the trend. When the stock is in an uptrend, you get positive news—and when it's in a downtrend, you get negative news. In the best-selling book *The Black Swan*, Nassim Taleb describes a Black Swan event as the following:

1. It is unpredictable.
2. It carries a massive impact.
3. After the fact, we concoct an explanation that makes it appear less random.

Nassim is a smart guy for sure, but I prefer to look at all this stuff upside down. You can't live your investing life preparing and looking out for Black Swans. You can't predict them, and you can't live in fear of them. From my experience, Black Swans are explained better with trend-following rules. "Pigs get fat, but hogs get slaughtered." Take some profits along the way up, and don't average down.

Black Swan events include 9/11 and the tsunami in East Asia. Trying to explain them is futile, but those events did create new trends, and old ones died with the event. In effect, Black Swans both kill and breed trends. If you try to embrace this reality, you may not stop fearing these trends, but you may be able to focus on the events you can manage—such as those in your portfolio.

To trounce the averages you must stay with winning trades and welcome volatility. We often live in fear of losses. We are ashamed about them at some level. In the blogosphere, especially the financial blogosphere, we tend to speak only of our winners.

In the real world of money management, the easiest strategy to *sell* to other investors is one that produces very little volatility. Masked in this linear projection of profits is the risk of large loss or, as the experts say, collecting nickels in front of steamrollers. Shit happens after you buy a stock. Much of it is out of your control. Sometimes bad performance truly is just bad luck.

The purpose of trend following is to focus on the price, context, and catalyst to get a feel for where the stock has been and where it could go. Investing is not a science, but billions of man-hours have been spent proving it could be. I believe charts are a wonderful tool, but like any tool they need to be used properly and in the right context. I choose to trend follow, so looking at daily price charts makes no sense and bogs me down. I want to take in the whole picture, the biggest picture you can have of a stock. By doing so I get a feel for the company, the product cycles, the execution by management, the industry in general, and maybe the market itself.

For me, then, charts have little value. They add noise. There is a good percentage of investors who would tell you that charts and technical analysis are important to predicting future prices. I disagree.

For purposes of definition, "Technical analysis is the study of market action, primarily through the use of charts, for the purpose of forecasting future price trends" (John J. Murphy, *Technical Analysis of the Futures Markets*). If you search the term *technical analysis*, the on-line community has created a great database of links, books, and other information on the subject. Stock charts show us prices over time, so I will use them in this chapter to outline all-time-high breakouts and overlay charts with news and events that may or may not have affected the company, business, or stock. Trends can run a lot longer than you imagine—in both directions. They can also end in a heartbeat. At school, if you miss the bell, you might end up sitting in detention for an extra two hours. While the stock market does have an opening and closing bell, there is, alas, no one bell that says "Sell." However, if you get used to looking at stock prices over time, most importantly the ones you own, you won't be the last person out of the stock market—the person turning out the lights at Enron.

Pictures are worth a thousand words and all winning stocks look the same—they make a series of all-time highs. It's time we took a look at a bunch of winning pictures so you develop a feel for how this gets done and what a winner looks like. Of course, this is presented in hindsight, but if you look at enough winners you should get a feel for what I am trying to teach you. Each has a different angle of ascent and time frame for the move upward. The most important point to remember is that you will see hundreds more at a time in strong markets, where the indexes are climbing (uptrend).

Here are some pictures that further illustrate this point:

Taser (TASR)

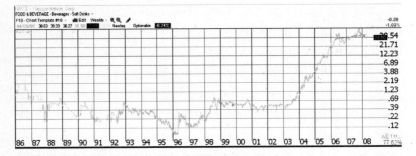

Hansen's (HANS)

Chicago Mercantile Exchange (CME)

Crocs (CROX)

M&F Worldwide Corp. (MFW)

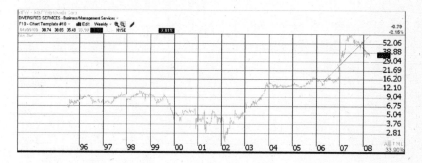

Google (GOOG)

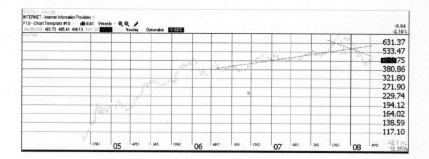

Baidu (BIDU)

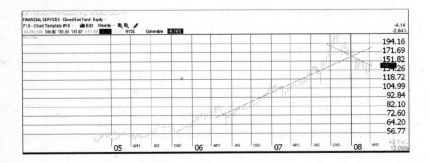

Garmin (GRMN)

China ETF (FXIO)

China Life (LFC)

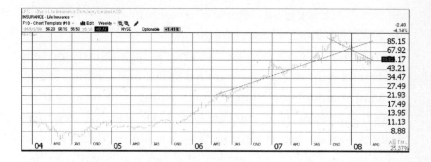

A Boring Winning Idea: CME Group

Market makers print money (See Chapter 9). The initials CME stand for Chicago Mercantile Exchange. This is one of the best-performing stocks nobody has heard of. It became a publicly traded stock in 2002, opening at about forty dollars and rising to over six hundred in 2007. It is a global twenty-four hour financial exchange for trading futures and options—things such as cattle and oil. If you don't follow all-time highs you probably would have missed CME, where it showed up at least four times in 2007.

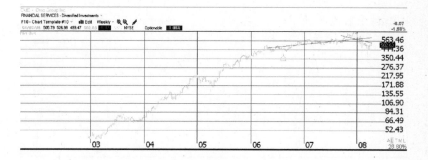

You don't have to be an expert to see that CME hit an all-time high back in 2003—and it didn't stop. It hit a new all-time high every two or three months, just like clockwork. They were obviously executing and there was obviously an increasing demand for their services. Your guess is as good as mine as to when this trend will end. CME is a good example of a company that, at least until late 2007, was doing all the right things.

Don't avoid a stock because the price is high. Ninety percent of investors want to buy one hundred shares of something or one thousand shares of something. What's wrong with owning three shares if your transaction costs are low? There is always an opportunity to own the best companies. Think about the dollar amount you invest, not about the number of shares you buy. If you had put twelve hundred dollars in three shares of CME in February of 2006, it would have grown to nearly two thousand dollars in the next two years. A lot of people who didn't want to buy a stock because the price was too high passed on Berkshire Hathaway, which went past $137,000 a share in 2007.

Alternative Energy Darling: First Solar

Solar energy was in vogue in 2007, and a lot of solar stocks started showing up on the all-time-high list. First Solar was one of the "hottest of the hots," and it was profiled on Wallstrip.

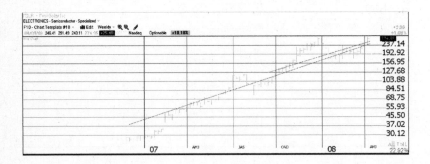

You don't have to invest in only companies you know, such as Google and McDonald's. At any time there are lots of companies that are executing well and growing. They just pop out if you watch the all-time highs. Then your job is to be unemotional and try on a bunch of them.

When looking at the all-time highs, remember that you can't own them all, and that there are great ones coming along all the time. First Solar looked like a great one in 2007. But profiting from sun fuel cells, complicated technology, and hybrid engines does not make sense to me. However, energy from the sun makes a lot of sense in that I understand the connection of cheap energy from sunlight. After all, every roof in Israel has solar panels.

So if you think solar energy can be adopted here, that is something you can stay with. The amazing upward price action in First Solar reminds you to follow price—not price targets—and arguments about whether it's overvalued or undervalued. First Solar was around thirty dollars early in 2007. Before the end of the year, it went over two hundred. Could anybody predict that? I couldn't. So stop predicting and let price be your final arbiter. That's how you catch a portfolio changer like First Solar!

No Reason to Sell: Research In Motion

I was flying home in 2006 and I heard the flight attendant say, "Turn off your cell phones and your BlackBerrys." The BlackBerry has become so ubiquitous that it is now its own category. It's not a phone. It's not a laptop. It's not your e-mail. It's your BlackBerry. It's become like Kleenex at this point—in a class of its own.

I must admit that I sold Research In Motion too early. It had gone up so much and I was lazy with my few remaining shares. I missed the meatiest part of the gain. In hindsight, it would have been fun to be around longer than I was. I judged it, thinking, *It was in the teens just a few years ago. I've made enough money.* I sold in the low fifties. It's a lesson. I should have been more thoughtful with my last few shares. The price had not called for any sell action. Maybe your last few shares of a big winner should be pried out of your dead, ugly hands by price.

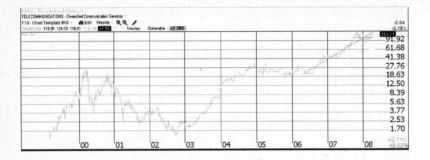

If you really have caught a trend, there's no reason to sell that last piece until it tells you to, until it just says, I'm done. I make this mistake all the time. It's lazy thinking. RIM went all the way to 135-plus and, looking back, I should have been buying more the day I sold it and then waited for my price stop. There are no shortages of lessons the market will teach you if you have lapses in discipline. This one was just one opportunity, fortunately: a missed upside.

Trends End

Investing is not all about winning. Trends end. To truly be successful over the long term, the trends that were your friends must be occasionally booted, kicked, and sworn away.

That's because those "friends" will take all your money when they turn. Fast. Many Wallstrip stocks, stocks I wrote deeply and passionately about in 2006 and 2007, had their trends halted and reversed in January 2008. If you search my blog in December 2007 and January 2008, you will see my personal battles and accounts of Garmin, Synaptics, Apple, and Amazon. The market goes through very difficult periods. There are always different reasons for downturns, always different catalysts, and always thousands of opinions from TV's talking heads. In hindsight, all that will matter little. What should matter to you is the price action of stocks in your portfolio and how you manage your positions through rough patches. Buying stocks as they push through to all-time highs is so much easier than selling stocks you have owned (regardless of time period) that looked fine one week earlier. I am with you here. It is brutal. Your mind will play tricks and your emotions will make it difficult to take losses.

Protecting the gains and minimizing the losses comes from recognizing that trends do indeed end. Some will stop, go sideways, and fall. Some will not only just stop—they will reverse overnight, and some will dance and trick you into believing they will go on forever before they rip your heart out. But they will end just the same.

The simplest explanation is that growth and margins have slowed, but while stocks are trending to the upside, there are sometimes subtle signals. However you decide to manage your profits on the way up, there is only one thing to do when trends in price end: just sell—sell completely and sell fast. It's like ripping off a Band-Aid. Once it's time, peeling it off slowly is not the way. You shut your eyes and let 'er rip! Furthermore, don't look back. If it was a mistake to sell and the company and price strength reassert themselves, you will see it again on the all-time-high list. That happens.

If you practice discipline and sell your broken trends, you will see many more opportunities. Remember, the stock market is all about endless opportunities.

Let's take a look at what trends look like when they have ended. The pictures tell it all. The news is built right in.

Beazer Homes (BZH)

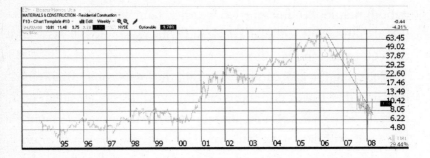

Palm, Inc. (PALM)

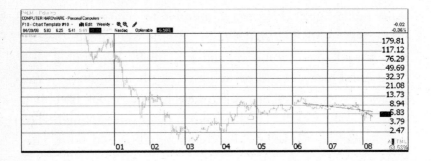

Crocs (CROX)

Ariba (ARBA)

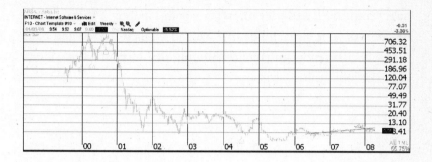

Lucent (ALU)

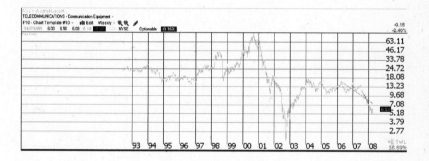

Sun Microsystems (JAVA)

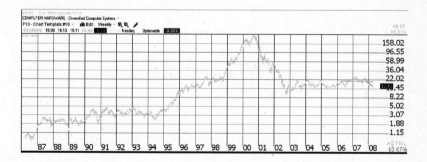

The stories, people, and industries are all different, but the results stay mainly the same. When long-term trends break, they rarely come back and they often get worse. Chapter 7 is important because it's your visual guide to what can happen—good and bad. Come back often when you are thinking that a certain stock looks cheap or looks too expensive.

To-Do List

1. The trend is your friend.

2. Black Swans will keep you up at night, but discipline is your only defense, so use it!

3. Linear profit strategies are a lie. With stocks and trend following, price volatility is a given.

4. A friendly stock and trend one day must be sworn off if price tells you to. Honor your stops. Trends end!

5. The stock market is all about opportunities. It always gets better, so stay in the game.

CHAPTER 8

Everlasting Trends

It is one of the great paradoxes of the stock market that what seems too high usually goes higher and what seems too low usually goes lower.

—WILLIAM O'NEIL

Despite all our technology and progress, human beings are wired rather simply. The physiological human needs (as described long ago by Maslow) have created the best (most consistent) investment groups of all time: Breathing, Sleep, Food, Water, Sex, Sleep, Homeostasis (living longer), and Poop (waste).

Information technology is a category that sticks out beyond the base of the Maslow hierarchy, but it has been one of the most powerful and profitable everlasting trends.

I keep an eye out for companies that fit into certain categories of these trends. Companies that do the best job within these categories will also do best in the stock market. To me, the key categories are:

1. Information: Knowledge, Power, Leverage
2. Vices: Tobacco, Booze, Gambling, Sex
3. War and Defense
4. Health, Wellness, and Vanity

Here's a close-up look at each category:

Information

We are addicted to information at a time when it has quickly become a commodity. The Internet, like the telegraph, telephone, railroads, and airplanes, has shrunk the world. Thomas Friedman's book *The World Is Flat* is an excellent read on the power of the shrinking world. Google has been the recent information company to shake things up and has profited like none in its past. Information is not a commodity if it is organized and delivered fast and distributed where you need it. For their ability to manipulate and organize data, Google (as of January 2008) is now worth more than Ireland, closing in on Exxon, and worth about the same as Berkshire Hathaway. That's big. Google could buy the *New York Times*, the *Wall Street Journal*, and several hundred-year-old companies and still have money left over. How did that happen in ten years?

Why Google Trumps Microsoft on the Web, Even if Microsoft Buys Yahoo

Scott Karp, a professional blogger, has a good explanation: "Google is a web-native company."

The main problem with Microsoft and Yahoo, looking forward, is that they are not Web-native companies—they rely on centralized control models rather than distributed network models, thus they are not aligned with the grain of the Web, which is fundamentally a distributed network. Microsoft does not have it and Yahoo does not have it. And if they merge, they still won't get it.

Microsoft and Yahoo rely on software lock-ins (Windows, Office, IM clients, Web mail) to maintain their user bases—but without distributing any of that value to the network or harnessing the value the network would give back if they did. As such, they do not benefit from network effects, which is precisely what powers

Google—and why Google will likely still beat a combined Micro-soft/Yahoo." Google has it. It's in their DNA. It's the Web.

Jeff Jarvis, another successful Web writer who has discussed the difference between Google and Yahoo many times, says it is diffi-cult to change traditional media business thinking. What drives the success of Google and other Web-native companies is completely counterintuitive to the perspective that drove the media business before the Web. Media used to be about tightly controlled silos; now it's about loosely affiliated, distributed networks. Legacy busi-ness can, potentially, evolve and survive, but only through a radical change in thinking.

The future of media belongs to Web-native companies—partic-ularly those who can innovate Web-native business models. That's what Google did with AdWords, creating a liquid market. Above all, the future belongs to companies that can leverage the network, becoming a network themselves.

The *New York Times*: A Great Brand but Doomed?

Let's take a look at the *New York Times* to further drive home the Web-native information and distribution problems facing old media. Without looking at a five-year chart of the stock and just reading an occasional story about Google and old media as to how it relates to advertising growth, you might expect the stock of the *New York Times* to be hurting. You would be correct, and their peak in price closely correlates to the IPO of Google.

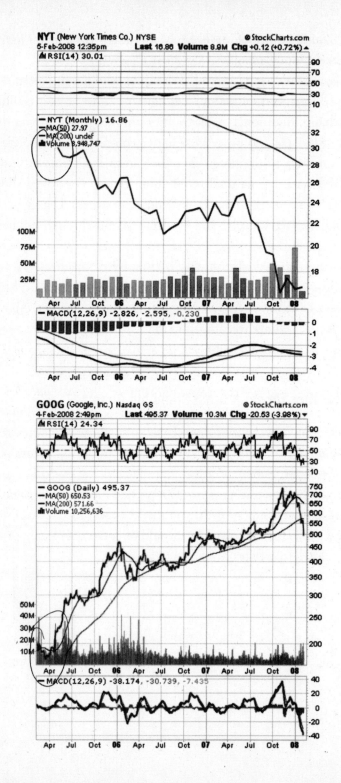

We could go through the business model, financials, and industry specifics, but it would be boring and painful.

Marc Andreessen, the founder of Netscape, sums up the problem in a blog post:

*Well, given that the Internet is the central force dismantling the
company's business, I'm sure that by now they've stocked their
board with noted Internet experts. Let's see:*

- *Brenda C. Barnes—CEO of Sara Lee; noted snack cake expert*
- *Raul E. Cesan—former CEO of Schering-Plough; noted Levi-
tra expert*
- *Daniel H. Cohen—president of DeepSee LLC, "an oceanic
exploration and submarine leasing company;" noted Jacques
Cousteau expert*
- *Lynn G. Dolnick—former head of exhibits for the National
Zoologic Park in Washington DC; noted marsupial expert*
- *Michael Golden—current publisher of the International Her-
ald Tribune; former head of the company's Women's Publishing
Division; noted sundress expert*
- *William E. Kennard—former head of the FCC; noted "seven
dirty words" expert*
- *James M. Kilts—former CEO of Gillette; noted smooth,
smooth shave expert*
- *David E. Liddle—here I have to take a pause as I actually
know this one; based on what's happening at the company, it
could be reasonably asked whether he's actually attending the
board meetings.*
- *Ellen R. Marram—former CEO of Nabisco; noted Oreo expert. Oh, wait, she actually ran an Internet company: "From
1999 until 2000, Ms. Marram was president and chief executive officer of efdex Inc. (the Electronic Food & Drink Exchange), an Internet-based commodities exchange for the food
and beverage industry." Ooh. I wonder if that ended well.*

- *Thomas Middelhoff—former CEO of Bertelsmann; noted expert on complicated family politics—well, that's probably coming in handy . . .*
- *Janet L. Robinson—current CEO of the New York Times Company; noted expert on horrific business implosions*
- *Doreen A. Toben—CFO of Verizon; noted 30-year debenture expert*
- *And finally, Arthur O. Sulzberger, Jr.—the Big Kahuna—the Man—the Guy In Charge—the chairman and scion—the dude with the cojones to actually defend Judy Miller. Not noted Internet expert.*

So, if you want to issue bonds to pay for FCC-approved snack cake manufacturing in a submarine on display at a national park by a sundress-wearing cigarette-puffing Levitra-popping Judy Miller, you're pretty much set. Go team!

Pretty funny, yes, but you get the point. Drastic times call for drastic measures if you want to disrupt Google's stranglehold on how the Web and information work in 2008 and beyond. You are either Web native or you are sucking the fumes of Web-native companies. Based on the board the *New York Times* has assembled, it will be hard to revive financial success of the *New York Times* brand from a newspaper model to a more Web-native media company. And it will be nearly impossible to stem the bleeding of advertising dollars to the Web.

Google also offers information to anyone, anywhere—from students studying late at night with no access to a library, to the corporate executive looking at financial statements at 11 P.M. researching merger and acquisition candidates. Google's services can be shaped and fitted to anybody's needs. It has become a market maker for words. Google "shrank" the world by allowing anyone to find almost anybody or anything anywhere. Google also leveraged the Internet, which is maybe the number-one most addictive thing

I can imagine. That also gave Google tremendous economies of scale and margin.

As usual, Umair Haque (www.bubblegeneration.com), a great thinker, had a thought-provoking post about branding in the Internet age (also on my blogroll). "Data as a Commodity" helps further explain the phenomenon of Google:

> *Data is inherently valueless in the edgeconomy, because it's infinitely replicable. Any structure seeking to limit access to data will simply be too radically inefficient for the market to bear in the medium-long run. So a massconomy strategy of "owning" a massive stock of data is destined to crash and burn. Rather, what is valuable is being plugged into (and plugging others into) the right flows of data. That's what Google does. You ask, I bid—flows. It's what Facebook refuses to do. And it's a small example of why media—in 2007, even new media—sucks. We can't reinvent industries if we don't think more deeply about their economics.*

This is good stuff, although I would argue that Facebook could realize this shortly (to be covered in Chapter 10).

Information is the most important everlasting trend because information gives people power. Obviously, Google leads the pack, but another great example of a company that benefited from this trend is Research In Motion (RIMM), creators of the BlackBerry, which allowed people to receive and send e-mail from anywhere. The first BlackBerry was an ugly piece of equipment, but it served an important function. The early adopters were stockbrokers, who used it to solve two of their problems. First, they could communicate information much more quickly because it was mobile. Second, it allowed them a channel of communication around the hierarchy. The financial industry is highly regulated, and the BlackBerry gave stockbrokers an unregulated back channel to discuss stocks and share information.

RIMM slowly expanded on that basic communication function,

but they also kept it simple. Parents liked it. Kids liked it. It was easy to adapt to. It crossed over from stockbrokers to ad execs, to nurses, to people in government. Those people liked it for the same reasons stockbrokers did: it's fast, simple communication from anywhere to anyone. Research In Motion has done a few things since the BlackBerry was introduced, such as improve the design. But the key element that got them over the top was that the BlackBerry became addictive. People get addicted to information just as they do to anything else. We are, most of us, information junkies. No matter what industry you are in, information does give you an edge.

Shrinking the World

A percentage of every investor's portfolio should be in products or services related to shrinking the world. These companies do one or more of three things:

1. Offering those products or services
2. Leveraging the existing network infrastructure
3. Helping people live in a constantly shrinking world

The most explosive way to add value to a portfolio over time is to tap into the businesses that are doing these things. Google shrank the world by bringing people together with other people, with products, and with services and information. It also benefited from the shrinking world by building on top of the telecom infrastructure, and it helps people live in a shrinking world. Google did all three. It made a market in data. Market makers print money.

For companies that do those things best, profits are insane. Anything that is involved in the shrinking-world trend will increase commerce, and anything that increases commerce will drive revenue and profit. Railroads, airplanes, and the telegraph come to mind. Companies like Western Union and Federal Express are good examples. Some of the wealthiest people of all time have been in the business of shrinking the world.

Shrinking the world means enabling people to connect with one another, or products to move better, faster, and cheaper. That might mean that Howard Lindzon can meet his Chinese counterpart on-line, and read his profile and think, *Holy smokes! We're interested in the same things.* Or he could find me. Now the product I create could be distributed in China. He thinks the way I think, and he understands the market in China, and he sees that my product can be successful there. It's done—imagine Wallstrip in Chinese! As recently as 2000, you could not easily dream, yet alone execute your idea, globally.

The shrinking world was really good to GPS (Global Positioning System) companies, companies that became the rage in 2006 and 2007 and persisted on the all-time-high list. I started writing about it in 2005, pointing out that GPS was available on cell phones, it is easy to use, it was becoming standard equipment in higher-end cars, and it was available in rental cars as well. People coming from the U.K. to the U.S. who rent a car to drive across the country no longer need to get maps. They turn on the car and it talks to them and tells them where to go.

For twenty years before that, mapping had been a big thing. Microsoft was one of the first companies to offer mapping soft-ware. For a few hundred dollars you could drive around with a map that you printed at your PC. Now it is free. If you go to Google Maps, you can even zoom in on your home. You can now do this from your phone if your car does not offer the service.

GPS has many applications and has rather quickly become ubiq-uitous. Once price declined, mainstream adoption followed. It was a trend helped along by a shrinking world. Satellite companies and software companies also profited. Major companies like Nokia paid billions of dollars to integrate products from start-up companies into their cell phones and give those things away as part of the cost of their hardware or services.

On-line collaboration is another trend in the shrinking world. Let's look at the big picture. The time is now. We have proliferation of cheap bandwith, open-source software, cheap hardware, and, most importantly, demand and the urge to connect. It's the pen-pal phenomenon on steroids.

Who is going to be the budding Apple in this space of on-line collaboration? Could it actually be Apple? Facebook and MySpace are the big early leaders. Google is definitely after the prize as well.

Vice

To be honest, most investors need look no further than a good list of vice stocks. In fact, if you have no ethical concerns about owning these businesses, just do it. Vice stocks are part of an incredibly strong everlasting trend: tobacco, alcohol, sex, and gambling are the best examples.

In fact, FocusShares has created a sin-based ETF. I will give you two chances to guess its three-letter symbol.

The hottest vice sector today is on-line poker, where a fourteen-year-old math whiz in New Zealand who can scrape together an entry fee can play on-line poker against the CEO of a major corporation. There are no significant barriers to entry, and the play can be anonymous. It is a frictionless, viral game and is now a multi-billion-dollar business.

There are tournaments, and the same person will not win all of them. It is almost impossible to do that. Roger Federer can run for five years as a tennis champion, but in poker the winner might be a high-school dropout, a nineteen-year-old piano whiz, a truck driver, or almost anyone with math skills. Casinos are being built across the United States and now you have Macau in China. People love to gamble. It is impossible to stop, and pretty much recession proof.

The "arms" dealers to the casinos have been some of the best-performing stocks ever. International Game Technology (NYSE: IGT) is a stock I own and we have covered on Wallstrip, and IGT supplies a majority of the slot machines around the world. WMS Industries and Bally's have been hugely successful as well. The buildup of Macau in China has obviously helped extend their growth.

The worldwide love of video games has been very good for companies such as Nintendo, Sony, Electronic Arts, GameStop (retailer), Take-Two (subject of a $2 billion bid from Electronic Arts), and Activision (now Vivendi). I love this industry because the subculture has been accepted. The innovation unleashed by the best-selling game Guitar Hero will push the industry into yet another hyper-growth period. Harmonix, the game's creator, has taken game interaction to the next level of creativity. All the video gaming companies above have been profiled at Wallstrip. These companies are only limited by the creativity of the people, as our shrunken world has created a global marketplace. The proliferation of the Web and the addictive nature of games and immersion by kids have created a huge demand for on-line multi-player games as well. Strangers play against each other over the Web. There is no money wagered (not legally yet), but the stage is set for fast growth as companies chase a share of the increasing pie.

Sex, ironically, as a vice has not been a very successful public market investment. It isn't well accepted in our conservative society, at least in the public and institutional financial world. The successful companies have not needed the spotlight to amass fortunes.

Furthermore, institutional money does not want to be associated with sex: "Oh no. I'm not going to invest in a fund that invests in porn!" In 2007 a friend mentioned Rick's Cabaret as an amazing investment opportunity. He explained that their model was simple: "Starbuckify strip clubs." The stock was near an all-time high, so I was intrigued. In fact, we Wallstripped the company. When you think of that kind of business, you think of sleazy guys running a cash-only enterprise. You think of Tony Soprano. I did some more checking and loved the concept. In fact, institutions were accumulating the stock. The stock eventually took off to the upside and more than tripled from our date of profile.

Whether investing in porn is right or wrong, whether it is for you or not, there is endless demand for the products and services, and some of the very big companies in the next decade are going to appear from this sector. If we enter a difficult investment period, I am convinced that the venture capitalists will look to the pornography space for disruptive Web companies. Profits matter, the world is shrinking, and if we in the U.S. won't do it, someone else will. You can cross those stocks off your list for whatever ethical reasons you have, but if the name of the game is catching a trend, then you need to look at some public companies that are in the game of making money off sex.

Beware! There are definite risks in vice stocks. As any company gets bigger, new obstacles appear, and companies involved in vices have obstacles that others don't have. On-line poker was one of the biggest open-field enterprises in our time. It was stopped overnight by government legislation. It went from a hundred miles an hour to zero because the government said, "You can't open an account at these poker places." Regulation can kill business overnight.

Even Google would suffer if the government gets involved. No business model or sector is foolproof. Understand that occasionally the government does show up, or a class action lawyer, or a different administration that says, "Screw the tobacco industry," or something along those lines.

But in the end, vices are not going away. Your odds of finding winners among vice stocks are much higher than in other areas, so if you want to make money in the stock market over time, regardless of the economy and market, keep a good list of vice stocks. You can count on Wallstrip and my blog to keep you updated on this sector.

War

Sadly, a third everlasting human trend is war. In the stock market, war is a bullish phenomenon because it creates a movement of money that is unmatched by other trends. War mobilizes government, and governments print currency. Governments can write check after check that change businesses and business direction overnight, spending on new companies and on old companies and reviving old product lines.

Wars have historically led to surges in the stock market. Wars generate huge profits for the arms dealers, and therefore investment and trend opportunities. Fifty years ago the boom was about tanks and guns. Today it is about such things as aerospace, unmanned drones, Kevlar vests, imaging, and satellites. Technology and weapons have been a perfect combination for profits.

Wars always last longer than politicians promise. The Iraq war was going to be a seven-day event, but if you had sold Lockheed Martin, Boeing, General Dynamics, or Raytheon when Saddam Hussein's statue fell, you would have left great profits on the table When a war is over, defense stocks do not just slow down—they flat-out stop. Timing the end of wars and conflicts is not your goal; money management, including partial sales on the way up, will help you profit from the business of war.

Health, Wellness, and Vanity

People have been chasing the "Fountain of Youth" since the beginning of time. Egyptians wanted to live forever. Romans didn't want to die, despite the fascination with gladiators. With wealth comes an addiction to living.

There are two sections in the health, wellness, and vanity trend: products that need FDA approval and those that don't. I generally stay away from the former because there is too much risk. Exceptions would be companies that already have FDA approval and are changing the way we do things. Allergan (NYSE: AGN) is an example of such a company. Whether this is for good or bad reasons doesn't matter, because people have accepted Allergan's products. Botox, implants, and the ability to turn back time are just a huge area of growth and price is no object. Allergan's margins are fantastic, and the stock ripped higher between 2005 and 2007.

America is obese, and it is likely our own diets, not just our lack of physical activity, that are doing us in. The weight-loss stocks have been a wild ride. I am watching the space for new leaders all the time. WeightWatchers has been the steadiest and most consistent public market weight-management company. WeightWatchers now has an on-line presence for men. My doctor told me that men who weren't users of the product are now starting to use the on-line version. A company like WeightWatchers that develops great tools and real solutions will score points in the stock market. It could just be old boring baseline food companies that revives this category. Watching the all-time-high lists will let you spot trends in the space early.

I am particularly fascinated by the "sleep" industry. Since I started blogging in December 2005, sleep has been a regular topic and I have owned most of the stocks in the space. After Apple, sleep is mentioned in more of my blog posts than any other word. It remains a favorite topic of mine, and a favorite among everlasting trends, but I have blown everything I made investing in the category on sleep apnea tests, sleep machines, and Ambien.

Sleep has been a hugely profitable industry for investors. Sanofi-Aventis (NYSE: SNY), is the maker of Ambien, the first blockbuster sleep drug. I have owned the stock, but when Ambien came off patent, I sold. We also profiled Respironics (sleep machines—NASD: RESP) on a funny Wallstrip. ResMed is the other big company in the sleep-machines business. The stocks have been incredible long-term performers and in late 2007, Respironics was acquired at a large premium by Philips. Respironics is a great example of great things happening to stocks in uptrends. For investors, the industry of sleep will remain a money maker as America ages. In case you were wondering, Ambien works for me.

In Good Times and Bad: Sometimes Great Brands Go on Sale

I love certain brands that are now iconic: International Game Technology (slot machines), Electronic Arts (gaming), American Express, Federal Express, Altria (tobacco), and Goldman Sachs. They are true leaders in their respective industries, but sometimes they do get sold and sold hard. They are always on the tip of my tongue and I am always watching their prices in weak markets for an opportunity to add shares. I prefer to add these specific brands when they have fallen at least 25 percent from their all-time highs. I don't like paying up for their stocks because they do not grow as fast as they once did. In good markets, I prefer to own the fastest, best-trending stocks.

When markets suck, I look at established companies that are involved in everlasting trends that could be out of favor. In March 2008, one of those times arrived. I added American Express because of the "credit crisis" market meltdown. I would rather buy consumer brands like American Express when nobody likes it than when everybody likes it. Their growth will return. The brands have survived many credit and bear cycles. If you say the name of those great companies in a crowd, people nod their heads. Because those companies are mature and they own their niche, there is no reason to chase them when times are good, even if they do reach an all-time high. When things get bad and the hot stock with the fancy name starts going down, individual investors and institutions get nervous fast. Stodgy old companies stay stodgy old companies, but they generally occupy very profitable spaces.

To-Do List

1. If you are investing in Web leaders going forward, stick to Web-native companies.

2. Google is reinventing the way information is managed and served.

3. Software-as-service Web companies like salesforce.com are part of a new Web everlasting trend.

4. Don't forget vice, war, and wellness stocks. There are hundreds of future winners and even some oldies.

5. In bad markets, look for my familiar names on sale within ever-lasting trends.

CHAPTER 9

The Big Picture: Brains and Bandwith

Encyclopedia salesmen hate wikipedia . . .
And CNET hates Google . . .
And newspapers hate Craigslist . . .
And music labels hate Napster . . .
And used bookstores hate Amazon . . .
And so do independent bookstores . . .
Dating services hate Plenty of Fish . . .
And the local shoe store hates Zappos.com . . .
And courier services hate fax machines . . .
And monks hate Gutenberg . . .
Apparently, technology doesn't care who you hate.
—SETH GODIN

The information revolution, our quest for faster, cheaper, and more relevant information, has been very good to me and other technology investors. While Lou Dobbs (CNN Business) complains about outsourcing and open borders and economists argue about deficits, the American Internet industry thrives. It has thrived because of the huge margins it affords entrepreneurs and investors. The Internet will likely be our biggest U.S. export in terms of time and energy. It is hugely profitable. It is who we are. For all the so-called America hate, the world loves our culture. They like our service. They *love* our cheap U.S. dollar and are exploiting it. Our culture has tremendous margins and so does the intellectual property we create in offices around the country for the Web. The Internet and information technology are themes that never let me down, so it makes sense that I end the book speculating on what could happen as the revolution continues.

Like technology from the quote above, the markets don't care which stocks you love or hate, yet we get angry with stocks, the stock market, and ourselves for being wrong on a day-to-day basis. We want perfection. We want to know why our stock went down, not up, *today*. Nassim Taleb, author of *The Black Swan*, says that humans are hardwired to learn specifics when they should be focused on generalities. He argues that we concentrate on things we already know and time and time again fail to take into consideration what we don't know. We are, therefore, unable to truly estimate opportunities, too vulnerable to the impulse to simplify, narrate, and categorize, and not open enough to rewarding those who can imagine the "impossible." That's pretty simple, yet genius stuff. In a world of increasing complexity, connections, and noise, the best investors will continue to step further away.

Information Technology: Opportunity Always Knocking

Beyond economics and the stock markets themselves, it always pays to take a step back and look at trends that the venture capitalists are focused on and investing in. Once in a while, groups of the best and brightest get together to think outside the box in a big way. This is how the great companies are formed; they are created with the big picture in mind. At the 2007 AlwaysOn conference at Stanford University, Joe Schoendorf of Accel Partners, a group of highly successful venture capitalists in Silicon Valley, gave a speech full of interesting trend information. These are a few of my favorite discussion points:

- Everything is changing. Globalization will drive the next forty years. Change is increasing at an accelerating rate.
- To have a prepared mind, you have to know that shift happens, and happens exponentially.
- 1 in 8 couples who were married in 2006 met on-line.
- The number-one English-speaking nation in the world is China.
- There are 65 million active sites on the Web, increasing by 50,000 a day.
- The number of text messages sent every day is now more than the global population.

People everywhere are seeking connections. We are using the Web and mobile phones constantly and with more efficiency every day. And to that end, the next five to ten years will be driven by companies leveraging the connected network and social media to connect one another. It is not an outrageous speculation to believe that consumers will continue to flock to the Internet as they have done for the first ten years. Clearly, the venture capital money and Silicon Valley are important factors in the trend's continuation.

Venture Capital: Stay Up to Date on Trends and Trendsetters

If you want to invest in technology and the Web, the best place to stay current are the blogs of venture capitalists and tech aggregators like Techmeme.com. In 2007, venture capital investments hit six-year highs. The wonderful financial circle of life was working its magic. Over $29 billion was invested in 2007 by venture capitalists, the most since 2001 ($40 billion), with biotechnology, medical devices, software, and energy being the main focus (according to the MoneyTree Report via *Investor's Business Daily*). Of course, not all these investments will be fruitful, but the next great leaders in 2009 and beyond will definitely come from this crop of money. The pump will be primed for the next great leaders to take the public stage. While others worry about economic slowdowns, bubbles, and IPO conditions, the leaders of these newly funded companies, at least the great ones, will focus solely on the task at hand: to become our new leaders, to become the next Google. There is no reason to bet that the cycle of innovation in the United States and the rest of the world won't continue. Besides, if our country's great run is indeed over for good, what good is money anyway?

Venture capitalists forge change in the information-technology space by risking and investing the early money. The people whom I look to on-line have also thrown their energy into a Web discussion about technology that goes on at various blogs. The VCs often invest when there are just four or five people in a room saying, "Here's our technology." So knowing how they think and the boundaries they use will help you learn how to think about trends. Venture capitalists are not trend followers per se, but trend starters. They are paid and trusted with huge amounts of dollars to follow a different segment of the market, early adopters and trend spotters. They deal with many of the same issues that you will as common stock investors. As such, it is helpful to learn to think as they do about opportunities, dealing with failure, and managing risk.

I asked two venture-capitalist friends of mine, Brad Feld and Fred Wilson, to contribute their thoughts to this book. Feld and Wilson take great risks and have a track record of success. They are also willing to share good and bad investments, which is a rare combination. Sharing takes time. They live in the life cycle of a company much earlier than I normally do and have a much bigger risk-and-reward scenario as well. Their job is to look ahead ten years and say, "This one is going to make a great public company one day." They want to find companies with products and services that millions of people will one day (soon, they hope) use and derive great benefits from. I can explore further from their blogs because each venture capitalist has his own blogroll of people he likes to read. That is the beauty of the Web—exploring through links. We can leverage off others' knowledge base and peer groups.

If successful venture capitalists are investing heavily in certain themes, you should keep the industries and sectors in mind. "Our time frame is way longer than yours," Feld said. "I don't think about sectors or categories. I think about themes that are long-term dynamics, ten-plus-year opportunities that are based on very deep technological change or significant user or market behavior that I think is going to change." A venture capitalist's job is to move an idea along (while making money for their partners). They take a very different kind of risk with their money, being willing to go all or none. You, on the other hand, get the benefit of seeing how their investment is performing in the market. You get the benefit of liquidity. You can wake up the next morning and sell.

The Internet: Where Is It Headed?

Fred Wilson has taught me a lot about the intersection of venture-capital investing and the Web. These days, Fred invests only in the Internet. He says, "We are ten years into the medium now. If you look at newspapers, radio, and television in the first ten years, what you will see is that in the first ten years of any revolutionary new medium, that medium tries to be something that was before—like TV was radio for ten years. They basically took the shows that were successful on radio and sat in a studio and filmed them. Then, finally, people figured out how to do TV the way that TV needed to be done. In much the same way, the first ten years of the Web looked a lot like newspapers. So now we're starting Web 2.0. It is just people finally figuring out what the real Web should be."

Wilson is interested in innovations such as the programmable Web, the semantic Web, the mobile Web, and the social Web. The programmable Web allows services to be built on top of other services. He said, "I could build a service on top of Wall-strip, and then someone could build a service on top of that. Like Legos—you snap one on top of another on top of another." The semantic Web makes the Web smarter, allowing information to be shared and combined more easily. The semantic Web is really about leveraging existing information to create a better on-line experience for everyone today. My fund has an investment in a start-up called AdaptiveBlue, alongside Fred's fund, Union Square Ventures. Adaptive Blue wants to help everyone browse the Web smarter. Their approach is to teach computers about the everyday things in Web pages that we are interested in, like books, music, wine, electronics, and people. Adaptive Blue has taken a top-down approach. They have built tools that leverage the existing information to teach computers about those everyday things we want more information on. They deliver the experience through structured content, shortcuts, and personalization. It is early in the progress and adoption of the semantic Web, but the prize is high for the winners.

The iPhone is an example of a product that taps into the mobile Web. "In effect, you have a real browser with you all the time," Wilson said. And Facebook is an example of a service that taps into the social Web. "All of a sudden we're taking all this data that's been collected in these social networks and powering new applications." (More on these developments in Chapter 10.)

Technology: No Free Lunch—Distraction, Security, and Privacy

I have argued on my blog that the only free lunch in the world exists for banking executives. When times are good, they dine and lend recklessly. When times are bad, they keep their jobs and write down their bad loans. The economy suffers as they fix their balance sheet problems and hold on to their reserves. The Federal Reserve's job is to put money back in their pockets at a spread that gets them excited again so that we can repeat the process. Everyone loses but the executives themselves. For the rest of us, greed and fear lead to cycles. Technology investments are not immune to rotten periods. In technology, innovation is your friend and enemy. You build a business based on one set of code or revenue model, and in six to twelve months the platform of choice can change.

According to a recent issue of *PC Magazine*, over the next twenty-five years, technology will become firmly embedded in advanced devices that deliver information and entertainment to our homes and our hip pockets, in sensors that monitor our environment from within the walls and floors of our homes, and in chips that deliver medicine and augment reality inside our bodies. It's all about connectivity and instant information.

But all of these huge Web benefits, such as connectivity, will have their drawbacks. The first is distractions. I am confident that entrepreneurs will build billion-dollar businesses teaching us how to manage the distractions. I said in my introduction to this book that he who manages distractions best wins. It follows, at least to me, that since the majority of us "suck" at managing these distractions, betting on distractions is also a great business.

The second drawback is security and privacy concerns. For those who choose to participate in on-line commerce and social networks, we "freely" give up our personal data (or so Facebook and Google would argue), and 2007 was filled with tension about the rights to that data. There is, of course, an implied trust. History does not offer me comfort at this point. TransUnion, Equifax, Experian, and many other corporations that own our data have profited greatly from reselling it. If you check your mailbox and see all the junk mail with your name on it, you know what I mean. Why would it be different this time? My bet is it won't. You can hide out or participate, but if you participate you must understand the tools and services you are using and the pitfalls of sharing your information. Hundreds of companies will be built around the security and privacy theme. There is too much at stake, both good and bad, to let the government decide. I believe free market solutions will evolve. (In Chapter 10, I touch briefly on LifeLock.com, a first mover in identity-theft protection and a company I invested in back in 2006.)

Market Makers

I have long loved our next-generation market makers and have blogged about them at www.howardlindzon.com. The Internet removed a layer of friction that just poured cash into the coffers of early winners. I am always looking for these businesses on the all-time-high list. Inventory (yield management) and market making have been two very profitable sectors of the early Web. The matching of buyers and sellers or lessors with lessees was an instant billlion-dollar category and has never looked back.

I was an investor in two private businesses that help owners manage excess inventory. The first was Rent.com, which I chronicled earlier. In 2006, I also invested in GolfNow.com, which helped the owners of golf courses sell tee-time inventory to local golfers. In 2008, GolfNow.com was offering local, last-minute tee times in over fifty markets, including Canada, the United Kingdom, and Mexico. GolfNow was purchased in March of 2008 by Comcast (the owners of the Golf Channel). I am now an investor in limos .com, which helps limo drivers manage their inventory.

Google, the fastest and most dominant business of all time to date, matches buyers and sellers of *words*. Baidu is the Google of China, and through most of 2007, both Google and Baidu made historic gains for such young companies. In the scrap business (automobiles), I own Copart as of this writing (NASD: CPRT). The global secondary market for auto parts has boomed, and Copart built the Web clearinghouse that makes it a leader. Not a sexy business, but their Webification has rewarded shareholders.

The local and global job market (www.Monster.com), classifieds (Craigslist.com) and hundreds of dating sites (www.eHar

mony.com) do the same thing, but for people. This segment of market making has been hugely profitable since its inception. The value proposition has always been clear, as both sides save time and money connecting from a larger pool. Maybe the perfect wife or partner really is out there.

In the financial markets, the CME (NYSE: CME) and the NASDAQ (NASD: NDAQ) were two of my favorite stocks in 2006 and 2007. I owned them both starting in 2008 as well. Both stocks routinely hit all-time highs. The CME brings together buyers and sellers on the CME Globex electronic trading platform and on its trading floors. The NASDAQ Stock Market, Inc., through its subsidiaries, provides securities listing, trading, and information products and services. Remember *The Godfather*? Well, the CME and NASDAQ are the legal financial versions of skimming. Skimming can be a great business if you manage the cash properly. To date, management of both have.

At the beginning of 2008, Interactive Brokers had become one of my favorite stocks. Interactive Brokers Group, Inc., together with its subsidiaries, operates as an automated global electronic market maker and broker. It specializes in routing orders, as well as in executing and processing trades in securities, futures, and foreign-exchange instruments as a member of approximately sixty electronic exchanges and trading venues worldwide. It offers continuous bid and offer quotations on approximately 324,000 securities and futures products listed on electronic exchanges (source: Yahoo Finance). I use Interactive Brokers for managing my hedge-fund stock portfolio. I find the product amazingly functional and easy to use. Their reach, breadth of products, reporting, and costs are a perfect combination for large investors and traders. As I write, they seem to be perfectly positioned to profit from the shrinking financial world—a world that wants to trade and invest its new wealth.

Please Note: There is no perfect stock or industry. Even Superman had to deal with Kryptonite, and, along those lines, every stock and industry has vulnerabilities. When overall demand slumps, transactions eventually slump. Due to the global consumer trend and global consumer reach, demand for the most part has not been an issue. Most of the above companies keep the cost of supply at a minimum and have reaped giant profit rewards as they use technology to scale at minimal cost and profit from the expanded customer base.

Internet Video

Take a look at this chart created by Paul Kedrosky, a popular financial blogger:

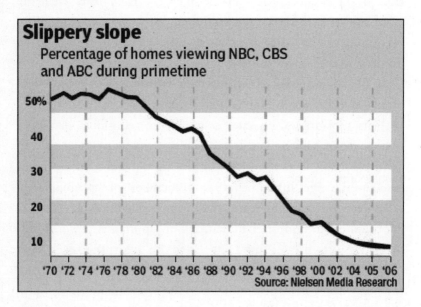

Slippery slope
Percentage of homes viewing NBC, CBS and ABC during primetime

Source: Nielsen Media Research

There is a massive audience defection away from network television. "Reality" shows have really been a boon for the networks despite the loss of audience, because they have stripped production and development costs right to the bone. The huge cost savings has in turn offset the dwindled audiences and advertising dollars associated with the smaller audiences. It will take something significant to change the trend at this point. But my experience in Web video leads me to believe that won't change anytime soon. It has never been cheaper to make and distribute video than right now! And it will get cheaper still.

People apparently have an inner need to be famous, to be discovered, and to share. Witness the unbelievable popularity of video sharing sites like YouTube.com (purchased by Google in 2006 for $1.6 billion). The industry has not fully exploded, because the monetization cycle has not kept pace with the growth. The advertisers are definitely moving dollars from television to the Web but are unsure how to spend their dollars in the most effective way. A sixteen-year-old's interaction with his or her laptop, watching user-generated content, is so very different from a "fat pipe" pumping in scheduled program with scheduled breaks. Serving advertisements effectively in the new medium is a holy grail for current leaders and hundreds of start-ups.

The lack of profitability has not stopped the creators, as low cost has trumped revenue potential to date. When I created and founded Wallstrip, I was making a bet on the industry, mainly that Google, Yahoo, Microsoft, or one of the Web leaders would develop the right formula for delivering relevant ads to my audience. As of 2008, we don't have *the* answer. But that has not stopped millions of people from making videos for viral distribution. Hope does not work in the stock market, but it could work in on-line video.

There is one big misunderstood fact about the on-line video business. Despite the low cost of creating and distributing Web video content, it has never been harder to build an audience. I believe that those who succeed will follow the path we blazed at Wallstrip.com; putting it everywhere. The content should be available where your audience is most likely to see it. It's a distribution model that CBS (our acquirer) and Quincy Smith (president of CBS Interactive) believe as well. Tools and services that help video-content creators build and monetize audiences will be big winners in Web video.

Medical

The medical world is due for explosive growth. With all the money pouring into venture capital and the cost of technology for research and development declining rapidly, I envision that billions in capital will go toward medical industries and the pursuit of living longer and healthier lives. The declining costs of technology and information have brought down the capital requirements for technology start-ups. Big venture capitalists are now competing with local "angel" groups on Web and technology deals. The ultimate payoffs are huge and, therefore, the large venture capitalists will need to allocate to businesses that need larger pools of capital and offer bigger payouts.

Furthermore, the medical industry is chaotic if not in total disarray. Mark Penn, author of *Microtrends* (a favorite trend book of mine), says we have a boom in do-it-yourself doctors (DIYDs). These people research their own symptoms, diagnose their own illnesses, and administer their own cures. Mark's research found that over the past forty years, retail over-the-counter drug sales have grown nearly ten-fold. Drug companies have taken notice of this trend. We can't watch television anymore without being bombarded by direct-to-consumer ads for pills like Viagra and cures for "restless leg" syndrome.

With the increase of DIYDs we will surely have other problems, including misdiagnosis. Web sites are getting better at providing medical information but information can do damage in the wrong hands.

The on-line brokerage firms that enjoyed a meteoric rise in the late 1990s turned cab drivers into stock traders. As I like to say, doctors are the new airline pilots. I remember as a kid that pilots were revered when they walked down the aisle. Now planes fly by themselves. Geez, there's even hope that someday genetic research will hand us a pill at birth that will correct our genetic defects.

The world has been awash in cash, gotten a taste of wealth, and truly wants to *live*. Intuitively, I would surmise that medical technologies, including medical instruments, drug delivery systems, and drugs themselves will be the focus of the large pools of venture capital.

Andy Kessler is a trend and technology writer whom I started following in the late 1990s while he ran an Internet venture-capital fund and wrote for TheStreet.com. He recently released a book titled *The End of Medicine*. His message is: Your doctor can't be certain what's going on inside your body, but technology can be. Embedding the knowledge of doctors in silicon will bring a breakout technology to health care, and we will soon see an end of medicine as we know it. Kessler has an amazing track record, not just as an author but also as an investor, so his thoughts and views are worth considering.

Spirituality and Wellness: It's Coming

I truly try to avoid discussions about religion and politics because on these topics I am out of my league. Furthermore, they always get negative. On the other hand, when I find myself in a room with spiritual people, yoga people specifically, I make fast friends. One of my best friends in Phoenix started At One Yoga and the Spiritual Gangster Brand. (I am an investor.) At One Yoga is the big yoga retail brand in Phoenix/Scottsdale. Ian has been on Wallstrip as we discussed the inevitable rise in eastern influence beyond the purely financial. It's about wellness, alternative medicines, yoga, and spirituality.

Although there are few pure plays today in the space, I believe hundreds will develop. I own Gaiam (NASD: GAIA) today, and it has been a volatile if not great performer for investors the last five years. Lululemon was an extremely hot IPO in late 2007. It's part of Wall Street's movement into this space.

Fashology: American Culture and the Internet

Oakley had an opportunity but missed. I believed their cool eyewear and brand would be a huge hit as technology and music intersected. I believe they have failed so far, but Luxottica must have seen the same opportunities. They purchased Oakley at a nice premium in 2007. I am convinced that consumers will never never buy Motorola or Sony sunglasses (maybe Apple), but we would buy Oakley glasses or Abercrombie jeans with Motorola, Sony, or Apple products built in.

The melding of fashion and technology is something that has fascinated me on my blog and on Wallstrip. Apple is the first big company to get it right. But they won't be the last.

Consumer electronics is mostly dead. Margins are brutal. I was driving past the high-end mall by my home in Phoenix and noticed that the Sharper Image store that had occupied the corner spot of the mall for the last twenty-five-plus years was closed. Bam. It was there three days ago. Now Sharper Image, the company, has been under siege and has recently filed for bankruptcy. Consumer-electronics retailers, including Circuit City, Incredible Universe (gone), and many smaller mall chains, have all been punished by the likes of Apple and the Internet distribution system itself.

Apple was the first company to perfect "fashology" with the iPod. Their computers were always elegant and make great furniture, but the iPod became a fashion statement. There is nothing radically different about competing products anymore, but the iPod continues to thrive in a commodity business. I am always watching the all-time-high lists for brands that are breaking out. As the price and margins of technology and consumer electronics continue to drop, expect fashology to drive many exciting trends in the years ahead.

Amazon and the Long Tail

From 1998 to 2000, Amazon and its stock were all the rage. That quickly ended in 2001 as the stock lost approximately 95 percent of its value. In October 2004, Chris Anderson penned a now famous piece for *Wired* magazine called "The Long Tail." Here is a brief excerpt from that wonderful article:

> *In 1988, a British mountain climber named Joe Simpson wrote a book called* Touching the Void, *a harrowing account of near death in the Peruvian Andes. It received good reviews but was only a modest success, and it was soon forgotten. Then, a decade later, a strange thing happened. Jon Krakauer wrote* Into Thin Air, *another book about a mountain-climbing tragedy, which became a publishing sensation. Suddenly* Touching the Void *started to sell again.*
>
> *Random House rushed out a new edition to keep up with demand. . . .*
>
> *What happened? In short, Amazon.com recommendations. The online bookseller's software noted patterns in buying behavior and suggested that readers who liked* Into Thin Air *would also like* Touching the Void. *People took the suggestion, agreed wholeheartedly, wrote rhapsodic reviews. More sales, more algorithm-fueled recommendations, and the positive feedback loop kicked in.*
>
> *Particularly notable is that when Krakauer's book hit shelves, Simpson's was nearly out of print. A few years ago, readers of Krakauer would never even have learned about Simpson's book— and if they had, they wouldn't have been able to find it. Amazon changed that. It created the* Touching the Void *phenomenon by combining infinite shelf space with real-time information about*

buying trends and public opinion. The result: rising demand for an obscure book.

This is not just a virtue of online booksellers; it is an example of an entirely new economic model for the media and entertainment industries, one that is just beginning to show its power. Unlimited selection is revealing truths about what consumers want and how they want to get it in service after service, from DVDs at Netflix to music videos on Yahoo!

This article was a real glimpse into the future of distribution and consumer demand. If you "Google" the terms *Long Tail* and *Wired*, you will find the full article. Trust me, it would be worth your time to read it.

My overall interpretation is that the little guy could still be screwed by the Long Tail, but that same Long Tail distribution and consumption behavior is now also unkind to the old guard and the highly paid media executives. All of a sudden, the little guy had this edge if he or she could tap it. (If you want to keep up with Chris Anderson and the Long Tail, he blogs at the following address: longtail.typepad.com/the_long_tail/.)

Whether Bezos and Amazon meant to or not, they have created an incredibly disruptive Internet company. I am long Amazon as I write.

Human Computer Interface: Big Changes Are Here

If you have not played Guitar Hero or Rock Band yet, you are officially *off* the grid. Investing is the last thing on your mind for sure. These games, along with the Wii from Nintendo, have created a newfound joy and enthusiasm for the gaming industry. Brad Feld and his partners at Foundry Group believe deeply in the human computer interaction (HCI) theme and are putting their money where their mouths are.

Here is a blog post from Brad's partner at Foundry Group, Ryan

McIntyre, himself a hugely successful entrepreneur (co-founder of Excite), angel investor, and venture capitalist:

The basic premise underlying our enthusiasm for the HCI theme is that the world of computing is ripe for a series of major shifts in user-interface paradigms. We've all been living in a keyboard-mouse-windows-GUI world for the last twenty years, and this paradigm has been responsible for the massive success and near-ubiquity of the personal computer.

But with the proliferation of new devices with substantial compute power (the computational might of an iPhone would once have categorized it as a super computer) and new "senses" supplied by accelerometers, touch-screens, digital microphones, cameras, we now encounter computing devices in our cars, on our nightstands, in our pockets, in our stereo cabinet, in our conference rooms and factories, at kiosks and screens in the mall and many other places. In fact, a 2003 study suggests that the average American encounters at least 70 microprocessors in the course of a day.

While we consider billions of PCs and mobile phones to represent ubiquity, true ubiquity occurs when something is so commonplace, it fades into invisibility in the background. Some have dubbed this idea pervasive computing.

In an era of pervasive computing, it is very often undesirable or impossible to interact with a nearby computing device via a standard Windows-based interface. (Especially if the device we are interacting with lacks a keyboard, mouse or display!). Thus we must be able to command our computers by touching their screens, simply gesturing to them, looking at them, speaking with them, or to get really sci-fi, by thinking at them. Freed from the confines of pointing and clicking on a two-dimensional screen to control our machines, we will see entirely new applications and capabilities emerge.

We can see current-day examples of these next-generation interface ideas embodied in the iPhone, Microsoft Surface Computing, the Nintendo Wii, Guitar Hero/Rock Band and many others. Notice that these innovations are applicable across numerous domains: mobile phones, enterprise computing and gaming. Any time we see an area with broad horizontal applications like this that runs across consumer and enterprise, we get excited because we smell "theme."

Brad further elaborated to me, "HCI has been around in the academic world for more than twenty years—in research labs—where people are trying to figure out ways to interact with the computer. I think that twenty years from now we'll look back on a mouse and a keyboard and have the same kind of reaction we had when we looked back on punch cards, which was a human computer interface for a long time."

In 1995 Feld made an investment in a company called Harmonix, two people who told him "that people should be able to use the computer to play music in a different way than they do today." Feld told them, "Fine, great, I'm in." Harmonix started working on trying to take some of the research they had done regarding music and computing in the Media Lab at MIT and turn it into a business.

In 2005, Harmonix released a game called Guitar Hero that became a cultural phenomenon and an overnight success. Feld explained, "They raised a little money and I think they were a $2 million or $3 million business until 2003. Then they were a $10 million business, and then they sold a billion dollars' worth of Guitar Hero, and their take of that billion dollars was about 20 percent."

Guitar Hero II also became hugely successful, and MTV bought the company for $175 million. Harmonix had created a totally different way of interacting with a video game. They started their business in 1995, so it took them eight years to become an "overnight success."

Feld told me that he believes there is so much opportunity for creating new companies in software and the Internet that his firm has decided not to try to do anything outside that, which happens to be their core expertise. He reminded me of a scene in the movie *Minority Report* in which Tom Cruise manipulated a computer simply by pointing at it. Feld said, "That's the killer app, making the user interface not constrained by a mouse and a keyboard. Making your interaction with the computer, whether it's the kind of thing Tom Cruise was doing or any interaction that you have with the computer, one that disappears into the background." Feld explained further: "I'm on the other line when you called. I'm talking to some other dude. I'm sitting in my chair four yards away from my telephone. What do I have to do to pick up the phone? Exactly the same thing I had to do fifteen years ago. I get up, I go over to my telephone, I press a Hold button. I press a button to answer your call. I answer the call. I say, 'Hang on one second.' You say, 'No problem.' I press the Hold button, and then I have to stare at my telephone to remember what to do to pick up the previous call. I've somehow managed to do that without disconnecting you. I finish up my previous call. I end that call and then I have to . . . it's just stupid. If I'm sitting in my chair, comfortable with my cup of tea, talking to some guy, why am I having to go through this brain damage to answer another call?"

Innovations will come to make the computer infrastructure smart enough to work in ways that fit with how you want to interact with tasks. I asked Feld what companies were in the lead in this area in the public market. He said, "Nobody. The public market is absent there. Privately there is a lot of interesting stuff within research labs at universities. There's some little, little stuff happening in the public market, but most of it's around video gaming." Feld believes that in the coming years the innovations will come from companies you haven't heard of. As a public investor focused on trends and all-time highs, I am following this area at Brad's blog.

I consider the iPhone, therefore Apple, to be an early leader in the space. I can use my fingers in a more intuitive way to see, grab, and organize data on my phone. This is surely a space worth watching closely.

Consumer Robotics

Have you heard of the Roomba? If you have not, chances are you will. When I interviewed Brad, we had a long discussion about robotics, specifically consumer robotics. Feld also offered an example of a company that he thinks he should have invested in but didn't. Brad knew a group doing pioneering work in the field of robotics, and in the late 1990s had a vision of building robotics for the masses. He said, "Way ahead of the curve, right? And they worked and worked and worked and got a few contracts, and did some work for Mattel, and built the business, and got some momentum."

Then they told Feld, "Look, we're thinking about raising some venture money. We have this vacuum cleaner robot that we think is going to be a huge commercial success on the consumer side." Feld looked at it and thought, *I don't know anything about robots, other than I know that there will come a day where people are going have these things all over the place, and I think these folks are really smart.*

Feld now says that the venture was worth taking a bet on as an investment, but because robotics wasn't a theme of his, he felt uncomfortable diving into it. The company, iRobot, ended up creating the Roomba, a robotic vacuum cleaner that drove significant success. iRobot came public in 2005 and continued to work on commercializing robotics. It took them fifteen years to get their science experiments to the point where they were venture funded.

Feld loves the Roomba. He said, "They are awesome. We have a house in Alaska, but we don't take our dogs to Alaska when we go there. We miss our dogs and to honor them, have named each of our robots after our dogs. You just turn them on and let them go around the room and vacuum the house. You can just sit there and watch and try to figure out what the algorithm is. It's fascinating to watch them."

I would look for iRobot to hit an all-time high before I was even interested, but robotics will become even more mainstream. That is not going away anytime soon, and I have my eye on it because I pay attention to Brad Feld's thinking.

Robotics is not just for consumers. Intuitive Surgical (NASD: ISRG) has been one of the "hottest" upward-trending stocks in the NASDAQ since 2005. They are the creators of the Da Vinci surgical robotics for open-heart surgery.

Oil and Alternative Energies: The Shrinking World Needs to Be Powered

You can't write a trend book during these times and avoid mentioning oil and alternative energies. This has been a mammoth trend for investors and as of this writing, no end is in sight.

As for alternative energies, the old-line energy companies have the power to make this happen in a bigger way than we have seen so far through 2007. Today, they are good at drilling, extracting, and moving oil. They are the companies to watch and to see if alternative energy is for real because they will make acquisitions if and when they have to. As I write, solar stocks have dropped 50 percent from their all-time highs, but optimism continues.

In truth, energy is an area I have generally avoided. There are so many moving parts to the businesses, and the government policies seem to play such a huge role outside basic supply-and-demand issues. I focus on the exchange traded funds in the space and the occasional industry leader to get exposure to the energy trends with greater diversification. I will sacrifice the huge returns for comfort as this industry is far out of my knowledge and comfort zone.

To-Do List

1. Technology does not care if you hate it—neither do stocks or markets!

2. We want to feel connected. The services and tools that make it happen will continue to lead in technology.

3. Pay attention to what the venture capitalists are thinking and doing.

4. It's not all about technology. Fashion has become an important factor in consumer electronics; Apple changed the game.

5. Market makers have a license to print money.

6. With respect to the Web, investors, consumers, and developers should focus on the programmable Web, the semantic Web, the mobile Web, and the social Web.

7. The human computer interface is changing—finally. Keep your eyes out in the medical space and consumer-robotic space for fast-growing leaders as well.

8. Oil and energy may be commodities, but the shrinking world needs to be powered.

CHAPTER 10

The Era of Social Leverage

Put that coffee down. Coffee is for closers.

— ALEC BALDWIN, *Glengarry Glen Ross*

Embrace the Opportunities

With today's tools for sales and networking, we should all be "closers," as Alec Baldwin demands of his sales crew in one of my favorite movies, *Glengarry Glen Ross*. (Of course, nutritionists would argue today that green tea would be a better reward than coffee.)

In the 1980s, when I started working as a stockbroker, I used index cards to keep track of my entire sales process. I remember when software contact managers came along. I became addicted to ACT! from Symantec. The index system gradually became a relic. In fact, we spoofed the age-old process on Wallstrip during our Salesforce.com (NYSE: CRM) show. Salesforce.com is a great product and an amazing stock-market success story. Simply put, it is customer-relation management software delivered through a standard Web browser. It's always open, so thousands of developers build features and services on top of it. You see, it's all about *leverage*. This kind of "open" leverage makes Salesforce.com difficult to value. It's one of the reasons why it has been a home-run investment inside a crowded space. But I digress.

When I made sales calls, I would get someone known as a "secretary," who screened the calls of the person I was trying to reach. People would tell their secretary, "Don't let any calls from Lindzon get through." At that time, the telephone was an easy device to screen, and anyone making a cold call was seen as a pest. If that were still the situation today, I might be the guy with the secretary. But it doesn't exist, and I am not that guy.

I now stay connected by checking my blog comments, e-mail, Twitter stream, or LinkedIn or Facebook page. I could force people only to e-mail me, but then I would never communicate with my kids (text) or my nieces and nephews (Facebook). Many teens just use their MySpace or Facebook page to stay in touch and up to date. In effect, by using SMS (text messaging), this new generation has completely bypassed e-mail. People who like Wallstrip, or who have been inspired by my work in some way (good or bad), can reach out directly to me through comments on my blog or follow me on Twitter. I am an active participant in the Web 2.0 society. Bill Gates may have somebody keeping his Facebook for him be-cause the super-connected and rich don't necessarily need or use the on-line communities. I do guarantee, though, that they must *listen*. The tremendous leverage possibilities have created a gigantic flow of money into social media.

Unlike Bill Gates, it is a good idea for me to participate. I was interviewing Jeff Pulver, the founder of Vonage and countless start-ups in telecom and the Web 2.0 space, for this book, and he has never been more excited about the opportunities. He has 3,800 Facebook friends, so he is fully engaged. He uses terms like "social branding," and likens the pre–social networking era to a flat piece of paper and refers to the post world as "the Galaxy." Jeff notes that "people are the winners as we get each other to take action and cause change."

Overall, the nerds call it social networking and the banks call it the "multiplier effect," but for my investment purposes, I refer to it as "social leverage." E-mail and now Facebook and Twitter have deleted an entire layer of friction, which was once symbolized by the screening secretary. A whole new level of networking will continue to evolve. Though most of the investing public does not use Facebook or has even heard of Twitter, they will.

Unlike financial leverage, which comes back to blow up financial markets, social leverage is proving all powerful. Those who tap it, manage it, organize it, and monetize it will be some of fastest-growing companies of the next ten years. Google has begun to invest heavily in the social networking space through its Open Social platform. The Internet leaders, as well as many new niche players and hundreds more in the pipeline, are involved in creating this leverage, which is the value that diverse people on the social graph can obtain from tapping into that graph. The term *social graph* refers to a global mapping of the relationships between people.

Social Leverage: Short History and Long Future

MySpace was launched in 2003, one year before Facebook, and soon became popular among teenagers. It grew mostly because it revolutionized what rock bands could do with their music. Bands flocked to MySpace because MySpace made it easy for its users to download music. MySpace was then purchased by media behemoth News Corp, and it has continued to flourish. Yes, there have been many losers in this early gold rush (Plaxo, Friendster, Tribe come to mind) but, again, this is just part of the process.

Bands on MySpace use the network to spread their songs, hoping to make them viral. The bands will continue to get smarter, adapt, and figure out a way to get around the middleman (record labels), because those that are successful have thousands of followers. They will get smarter at using the tools that are available to them. For example, they will have better information about where their fans are, and maybe put their tours in the neighborhoods where the fans live. Maybe they will visit one city four times instead of hitting every city.

The social network revolution leaped forward with college

students using Facebook for posting photos and communicating thoughts and locations. The third revolution? Who knows? But I can almost guarantee that by 2010 we will be leveraging ourselves socially in powerful and profitable ways. Politicians, for example, may conclude, Why would I spend money on TV if everybody I want to reach is on Facebook?

Inning One

I use the railroads for context in this case. In 2007, over 100 years after the initial boom and bust of the great railroad build-out, the survivors and leaders were hitting all-time highs. Railroads connected communities, and all along the new lines commerce flourished. The Internet had its tulips and railroad look-alikes, i.e. the telecom companies, such as Lucent, Nortel, WorldCom, Exodus, Qwest to name a few. But over the next 100 years of the Web, the commerce will unfold. It is borderless and infinite. We will look back at the information and social-leverage leaders of today and marvel at their growth and wonder why we did not stay invested and get reinvested in new leaders through the bumps along the way.

In late 2007, Microsoft invested $240 million at a $15 billion valuation for a tiny stake in Facebook. What took them so long? Were they crazy? Time would tell. In my opinion, the market immediately voted that it was not crazy as Microsoft hit a five-year high. The market said, You know what? There's finally a little hope at Microsoft. Will it stick? At the time of this writing, Microsoft was bidding for Yahoo and all the Facebook gains have evaporated, so it is very hard to declare a simple yes or no. Investors do know that $240 million is nothing to Microsoft, so it's a calculated risk.

In return for getting this stake in Facebook, Microsoft likely concluded, We'll give you your $15 billion valuation, but we don't want to put a lot of money in at that valuation. Facebook won because they got a high valuation, which they wanted as they moved toward an IPO, or maybe because they wanted to buy other companies. Microsoft also won in a way because they blocked Google from a move on Facebook. At the end of 2007 a potential war was heating up in this space. It will be a long war with many battles won and lost along the way. The stakes are just that high.

In 2008 and beyond, the social networks and the remaining portals will become the platforms that launch widgets and applications that the creators and their users can spread with little friction, virally, from one user to the next. Marketing and distribution costs will continue to drop. Those focused on creating destination sites will find it harder and more expensive to build an audience. The competition for eyeballs and audience has never been greater. And, yes, it will get harder and noisier for sure. While it has never been cheaper to produce content or distribute content, it has never been more difficult to build an audience. Those focused on the tactics of the early Web and old media channel building will be in for a surprise—in short, a major lack of interest and traffic.

Google and Facebook are proving that companies today can scale faster than companies before them ever did. IBM ruled computing for forty years. Microsoft ruled software for twenty years. Google has risen farther, and faster. It was the first to capitalize on the new infrastructure in a big way. Now along comes Facebook, which started in 2004 and gained 54 million active users and a $15 billion valuation in just three years. Google and Facebook leveraged the Internet infrastructure into something that became so viral it was impossible for the "smartest" financial brains to value them. By the time you read this, new players may rule. But with the niches this trend will create, and the resulting leverage a person like me (or you) can create, you need to start thinking that there are no boundaries to what can be done by someone with an idea and a will to succeed—from any corner of the earth.

The best-of-breed companies in this trend have incredible margins, exercise tremendous leverage, and all they do is take care of brains and people. They have no packaging, no shipping, and no production cost, so their product is seamlessly delivered and very highly scalable. Just as the railroads built infrastructure decades earlier, the telecom bubble of 2000 built an infrastructure, and so created enormous capacity. Now, technology and software are building upon that infrastructure. This is never going away. It will intensify. Technology IPOs will come from nowhere and global consumer brands will appear as if started yesterday.

The new Web and its toolmakers have created the "near" perfect platform for making connections and exchanging information and ideas. Although revenue is relatively light and profit starved today, I predict an industry littered with cash cows. Furthermore, social leverage is not likely to fall under government control. Everybody will eventually have access to it, so meddling governments will see human and capital outflow. As I pointed out in Chapter 6, a fourteen-year-old math whiz from off the grid, armed with money for an entry fee, might play at PartyPoker against the CEO of a major corporation. No edge, no friction. The U.S. government mucked things up for the on-line poker companies, but it won't be able to do that for long, and it will not have control in non-gaming areas. Businesses that are built using the social graph and social networks as their backbone will have endless opportunity. There are, and will be, thousands of new ways to get in the game.

For example, the "working retired" are using the Web to remain a relevant and fertile growth market as both producers and consumers. It is so early that it's hard to measure the productivity impact on a global scale. The working retired want to use the social-network tools and need to learn them. Thousands of business opportunities will present themselves. That's good.

At the beginning of 2008, the forty-plus-year-old category was the fastest growing on Facebook. They will also be the fastest declining if utility is not great and the noise continues to increase. This trend is socializing on steroids. But despite all the great opportunity here, there is the increasing noise that has no limits, boundaries, or defined utility for the masses. This is not necessarily bad, and could and should be good. The stakes are very high. Of course, time will tell.

Nothing Is Perfect

No industry evolves without problems. Social media and social leverage have made an attention-deficit society even more distracted. Distraction is indeed at an all-time high. Spam is also an issue. If you are not careful whom you befriend and how you filter those friendships, social spam is inevitable. Twitter is the best social tool I have used with respect to creating a spam-free social environment. Russell Beattie, an entrepreneur and blogger, summed up Twitter best: "It has almost a million members, a thriving community, lots of discussions and yet doesn't have spam or troll issues. Using Twitter, I only follow the people I want to listen to, just like I subscribe only to media I want to read. But the inverse of that is I only get to say stuff to the people who are following me—which means that if I am an idiot, I only get to bother those people who are stupid enough to follow me. The effect is sort of a decentralized moderation system."

FriendFeed raised $5 million in February 2008 to grow their version of Facebook's most popular feature, News Feed. They are relying on some extra features and the fact that it is "open." It works within Facebook. You and your friends each pick the sites you use, that you want FriendFeed to track for you. Then every activity is presented in a running stream, with every item from all your friends appearing in chronological order on your FriendFeed homepage.

Monetization is, of course, a huge issue as well. Google has profited most to date. Most of the social-network inventory (pages) are difficult to value, so it's valued at virtually nothing. I am betting we will solve this problem soon. Why?

Take another look at this TV Network audience chart from Chapter 9:

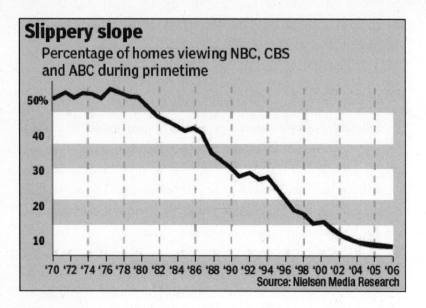

The viewers are leaving, and with them go the advertisers. Those dollars will make their way onto the Web.

I am putting my money where my mouth is. I am making private equity and venture investments in this space because I believe we will figure it out. The flow of eyeball and advertiser traffic onto the Web is too great to ignore. Existing leaders and start-ups are focused on building the tools to help syndicate and monetize the content better.

Leverage Yourself: The Era of Personal Branding

A high percentage of social-network participants are just voyeurs. They don't participate, but they are watching—your friends on Facebook checking in without you knowing; it's addictive. They have binoculars into your social being. The old movies revolved around neighborhoods and the people within a local community. We peeked into the small communities and enjoyed "the slice of life." Social networks like Facebook have exploded the neighborhood and binocular reach. Don't just watch it, though—get involved!

Jeff Pulver calls the social branding opportunities "life equity." Most of you will doubt the power of this, so let me give you a great personal example. When I wanted to become a better investor, I was drawn to the blogs of venture capitalists. I discovered many blogs that I loved, and Fred Wilson's was at the top of the many lists. Through his archives, made possible by search, I accelerated my learning curve. We shared the same passions for family and the Internet, except that, as an Internet investor, he had been to the Super Bowl. He was an MVP in his field. I slowly got involved in the conversation at his blog. When he blogged in 2006 that he would be in Phoenix, I offered him and his son two tickets to a Suns game. He tells a funny story at his blog that, where his family was concerned, I was a stalker, but Fred knew me from the conversation at his site and could find out more about me at my personal blog. Due diligence was sped up. Flash forward a few years: We have become good friends and not only was Fred an investor in Wallstrip, but we continue to leverage each other's network and make investments together.

Here is another example of the leverage possibilities. Until recently, if you wanted to come to the U.S., you had to pack up all your possessions and set yourself up legally in the new country, and even then there was no easy way to have your talents known. Until just a few years ago, you might have to take a different type of job than the one you were trained for. As the Internet shrinks the world by widening the talent pool, today's job seekers and the people who might hire them meet at electronic hubs like Monster. com or Craigslist.com. Job hunters today can browse the global-opportunity job market before moving. An entrepreneur in Eastern Europe, Asia, or Russia who trusts his programming skills knows that with Craigslist, he can buy a one-way ticket and find work. Shit, he or she can just work from home in Eastern Europe, India, or Asia, for that matter, because they have better bandwidth.

The social leverage gained from social networks depends upon how people use it. It is an individual experience. An eighteen-year-old uses Facebook for entirely different reasons than a forty-year-old. An eighteen-year-old asks, Where should we go to eat? or Who else is studying this or that subject? Most forty-year-olds are still at the stage where they say, I don't get it. For those who do, you can use Facebook or a personal blog to market your services from your home long after you would have retired.

Jobs and dating are two of the biggest profit areas in the social-leverage space and the Web in general. People will definitely pay for these connections from both sides of the table. Furthermore, from a global people pool, a person is more likely to find a perfect match—be it in a job or a date.

Leverage Your Business

Social leverage also provides tremendous opportunities for businesses. Wallstrip is a great example. I had a simple idea and pulled together a diverse crew of young, talented people. We piggybacked on the existing technology and infrastructure with a plan for a show about stocks in trends. Unless you have massive capital behind you, creating content is historically one of the riskiest start-up businesses because it is very hard to leverage. You have to create it, you have to spend the money on talent, you have to edit it, you have to distribute it, and then you have to find advertisers. All the while, you must keep the talented people together. I dreamed up Wallstrip, and others got involved, for the leverage that we could create in our specific fields. I wanted to become better known in the financial world, and to write. The producers and actors were looking for a cheap, smart, frictionless way to leverage their talents and to be discovered.

We used the tools available on the Internet: YouTube, free video hosting, and syndication tools like FeedBurner (purchased by Google) and TubeMogul (I am an investor), WordPress, all open-source software products. Wallstrip showcased our talents, but we used the tools to become known experts in our fields at a fraction of what it would have cost just a few years ago. It was months—not years—before people began finding me. Ten years before that, if I had wanted to write for TheStreet.com and get paid for it, I would have had to send in a few articles and get the attention of the managing editor. Now, someone at TheStreet. com sees Wallstrip, decides it has value, can syndicate the show with a piece of code, than ask me to write for them, increasing my audience and reach and that of Wallstrip once again. They win, too, if their audience likes what we have to say. The fast track to TheStreet.com as a writing gig wasn't a possibility as recently as 2000. It would have been a waste of time, for the return it would have made, for me to reach out to TheStreet.com and say, "I want to write for you."

Any idea or business has that kind of leverage today if they have a thoughtful, meaningful message, product, or service and it becomes viral. The toolmakers who help and allow businesses to monetize that value will profit handsomely as well. They own the data of all this digital shuffling. It's extremely valuable, if history is any guide.

Invest in Social Leverage

MySpace.com was the first company to cash out in the social-networking space. Facebook is today's hot company, garnering media attention and corporate love (advertising dollars). Will Facebook become the Google of social leverage? I am not sure, but at the end of 2007 the market was saying, and Microsoft was saying, that social leverage was a new frontier. We are in an investment environment where you want to be investing in businesses whose values are hard to measure. That's your continued edge, and more companies are going to benefit.

Is "Free" the Death of the Web?

I say no. I have investments in LifeLock.com, TubeMogul.com, BlogTalkRadio.com, AdaptiveBlue, Disqus, and V:social. I have already seen exits in Wallstrip.com, MyTrade.com, Rent.com, and GolfNow.com. Today's big services like Facebook, MySpace, and LinkedIn are growing like wildfire partly because they are free, but they are gathering an incredible amount of data and information. We are freely giving up our religious beliefs, our ages, where we went to high school and college, our jobs, and so forth, to these companies. There is a given level of trust that seems incomprehensible to some. Some people are saying, Facebook could be an evil company because they might use that data against you. To which I say, There is no such thing as a free lunch.

Using services like Facebook or Twitter, I am marketing myself to a massive group of people. If I didn't put that information out there, why would anyone out in the digital universe be my friend? Why would they trust me? If I can't figure out who they are and why they want to be my friend, why would I want to be their friend? If you use social leverage, you have to give up that information. You do have to be careful, of course.

New industries will be spawned and billion-dollar businesses created to monitor and try to protect your information and identity as it goes digital. In 2006, I invested in a start-up called Life Lock.com. The premise was that your identity would eventually be stolen and you needed to protect it proactively and insure yourself against the potential harm. In 2007 and 2008, the company was already highly profitable, with over $40 million in capital raised. The Web created a multi-billion-dollar industry and potential billion-dollar business—overnight.

Because the social-leverage trend is in its early innings, you will need to think about the growth from leverage opportunities like never before. Facebook is probably the number-one story dominating tech news today, even though it is not yet a public company.

There is a fascination about Facebook today like there was about Google for the last three years. Just as in tennis, where the sports media tries to create rivalries between players such as Andre Agassi and Pete Sampras when there isn't really a rivalry, investment media is trying to create a rivalry between Google and Microsoft. Wouldn't it be more fun if there were a worthy competitor to Google? A lot of smart people put their money where their mouth is, saying that Facebook is not overvalued. The overvalued camp will tell you, Well, money is cheap and venture capitalists are stupid and we have this bubble mentality, but let's look at it from the other side. There are so many market opportunities that weren't possible a few years ago for most companies, both new and old.

While most consider *bubbles* a bad word, I am with Daniel Gross, longtime financial author who penned *Pop! Why Bubbles Are Great for the Economy*. A few years ago, Facebook was in the same position as I—or as any start-up, for that matter: they simply had an idea for a product. It is now the centerpiece for reaching out and talking to other people. I doubt that it will be Facebook ten years from now, but there will be hundreds of businesses built on it, just as after everybody bought an iPod, billions of dollars of accessory sales were generated and many companies spawned to capitalize on the trend. Take a pass on this trend if it isn't for you. I have no doubt that you can make money if you stick to the everlasting trends listed in Chapter 6, but as Daniel Gross hypothesized, I believe the telecom boom and bust was good. It set off a longer-lasting global information boom.

Brains and Bandwidth

There is now a way to build a groundswell like never before. Three years ago I dreamed of writing. Now I have 4,000-plus subscribers to my blog. I started with a simple, free piece of software (Word-Press). Nobody was listening. Consider Wallstrip's 10,000 subscribers, and probably 30,000 people a day watching our three-minute show. No marketing, just blogging, linking, and participating in the conversation of leading thinkers in the Internet space. Consider the leverage that I was able to attain as an individual talking about stocks from my office and from my hotel room on the road. The leverage was created without employees and the aid of a PR firm.

Using the tools of social leverage, there are all kinds of things you can do from your desk. I live in Phoenix, yet I project myself all over the place and all at one time. Book authors have always gone on book tours. Today, there are tools and services like Blog-TalkRadio. Using a mobile phone, I can create a live talk-radio show instantly. People from all over the world ask me questions about my book, stocks, venture capital, or just chat about sports. It is expensive for book publishers to fly authors around to Barnes & Noble stores or for studios to fly actors on movie press tours, but I might do fifty days in a row at the same place and time on a live Internet radio call-in show, and that becomes my book tour. The costs saved by the publishers could just flow to the tool providers providing the savings as more commerce gets created.

Faster and Steeper

Today's trends act different. They seem steeper in both directions. Shorter product life cycles and increased global competition for good ideas are likely the cause. Furthermore, we have shrinking attention spans. For companies, though, a global reach may extend the brand and the companies themselves. By steeper and faster, I refer to revenue growth, profit growth, distribution, and stock performance. For example, Crocs became global seemingly overnight. Ten years ago, they would not have had a Web site and might be selling in their home country or community. A manager with ten years of experience working on expanding McDonald's in China might go to a start-up at Chipotle and help them do the same thing in one year. Not long ago, I might have thought that opening 600 U.S. stores was impossible for a company such as Apple. Now it's a global possibility. A few years from now, when the U.S. is saturated, Apple may be just starting to tap into emerging markets. For the truly great companies, trends can persist much longer than they once did because there are bigger possibilities in this "shrinking" world. Let price, not valuation, be your arbiter in the end.

My gut feeling is that there will also be more flame-outs than in previous cycles because products, if the company executes, will get to a saturation point much more quickly. Successful ideas and companies will also attract competition faster. Ten years ago, start-up costs gave companies with a good idea more time to execute. Nowadays, regardless of profitability from an innovator, competition is heavy. If companies don't execute, they will flame out faster because investors will run from products and stocks that don't catch on.

Trends are evolving faster and steeper because of the shrinking world, because of the mobility of the workforce, because of services that tap into the shrinking world and our knowledge leverage from search engines and other Web services and tools. Crocs leveraged themselves through social media. Chipotle leveraged McDonald's knowledge of systems and capital to expand lightning fast. Chipotle grew partly on the knowledge base that McDonald's had built up for many years.

Traditional financial media is going to call companies like these overvalued because social leverage is new to them. I would argue that, because most analysts don't understand social leverage, they don't acknowledge the leverage available from such things as Internet search and from far better informed management teams. Managers can create companies that are built for faster growth because of a new ability to leverage knowledge and customers.

So many industries have been disrupted. Travel agents—gone; stockbrokers—washing cars in Morgan's private wealth department; newspaper classifieds—Craigslisted. Real estate agents don't see it, but they are done as well. As Al Pacino would say in Scarface, "Say hello to my little friend"—Zillow.com. The charity business has been turned upside down with Web tools. Microlending (Kiva.

org and DonorsChoose.org) are changing the way loans and charitable donations are made. Social networks may create whole new revenue streams for charities. Tiger Woods will think, *You know what? I'm out there on Facebook and I want to give $100,000 to charity for the next four people who can figure out how to befriend me and engage me in a conversation. You pay me $100,000, you get to play a round of golf with me, and the money goes to charity.* A pro athlete may Twitter the action from the dugout or the sidelines. We may no longer need play-by-play analysts if the players themselves can broadcast. There are just so many possibilities.

Search itself will evolve. We all use Google or one of the search engines to find information, but "discovery" and "social search" are increasing in importance. eBay spent over $70 million to buy an early leader in the space called StumbleUpon (www.stumbleupon.com). It is no longer good enough just to present all the world's data, you must help me find why it's relevant to *me—now*. I don't just want suggestions because I will pay for exactness. Time is money—my money.

I am not going to be so bold as to say that Facebook will or won't be a megacompany ten years from now, that it will be worth $5 billion or $100 billion. They have much proving to do, and the private valuation has increased the pressure to succeed and create profits. What you should be focusing on is the all-time-high list and the blogs mentioned here and on my site. There will be hundreds of companies showing up over the next two or three years who leverage social connections to build sales and brands. The great consumer-product companies and start-ups of today will use social tools to explode their products and sales into new categories and global markets at a rate not seen before. Keep some cash available and your mind open to the possibilities.

You Can Do This: Have a Positive Attitude

I have now come full circle, back to the opening chapters of this book. There is TV, which is noise. Turn it off. There are headlines, which will make you zig when you should zag or do nothing. The only headline that matters is the all-time-high list. There is a mountain of commodity data about any stock in particular and about the market in general. Understand that the stock price today is where it is because a lot of brilliant (and dumb) people have factored all (or none of) the data into the price.

With the proper attitude, one-hundred-dollar oil is an opportunity, not Armageddon. Watching how the market behaves with hundred-dollar oil will alert you to the possibilities of solar stocks that were littering the all-time-high lists in 2006 and 2007. Instead, you would have caught oil and solar stocks by asking, How do you make money if oil is at a hundred dollars?"

Your job is to ask, Is this something that would fit my investing style? Is this something that can continue? You have read little in the way of conventional wisdom about investing in these pages. There is no buy-low-and-sell-high advice. There is no advice about valuation, except to say that it only matters when it matters, and that when it does matter, it is too late. I have tried to show you an approach to investing that does not rest on traditional ways of thinking about investing. My approach rests instead upon trend following, on less is more, one idea a day, all-time highs, money management, leveraging a connected and trusted network that you can build yourself, and opportunity.

Find an investment-entry strategy that works for you and focus more time on money management. You need to have a plan, but you can do this investing stuff yourself. Lindsay Campbell, Wallstrip's original hostess, is proving it with her stock portfolio. She does not have a broker. Never has. She understands the importance of cost control with respect to commission and trading. She had never heard of a stock before Wallstrip, let alone bought one. You might call her lucky, but I think she is smart. She is finding ideas that are in tune with her thinking and stocks that are trending. We talk about her stocks and she knows I will kick her ass if she buys "rumors" and stocks that are not my favorites. I remind her that stocks go down. It's not always easy.

Rose, who works in my office, has been patient and has bought the best stocks in positive trends that she could understand. She has been printing money. Most importantly, she is learning the word *sell* from me. Here is what I think Rose and Lindsay have done right: They found someone—it happens to be me—whom they know they can reach, either through the Internet or direct contact, whose interests are aligned with theirs. They have taken baby steps, they have been very selective, and they have been diligent about the stocks they decide to own.

At the moment, they are beating the stuffing out of me and every mutual fund they might have chosen. They are doing so with a fraction of the effort. They are not glued to CNBC or checking stock quotes all day. They are leveraging their social network. Yes, they will make mistakes. They will occasionally get lazy. The market will "taketh away" and challenge their faith in stocks and their discipline. If they don't get too lazy, they should build their net worth and enjoy the stock market, the best part of capitalism America has to offer.

To-Do List

1. Take advantage of social-leverage opportunities to leverage yourself and your business, and to do your investing homework.

2. Set up one social-network account and make some friends or find old ones. You will have fun. Go slowly.

3. Experiment with new Web social products. Read about them at Techmeme.com and follow the thought leaders I introduced.

4. Focus on the opportunity; the glass is half full.

5. Less is more—build lists, trade less, stay in the game.

ACKNOWLEDGMENTS

So many great people helped me get inspired to finish this book.

Most important for me is my wife, Ellen. In 2002 I was washed up. I was *en fuego* IN REVERSE! My wife coulda/shoulda kicked me when I was down. Instead she just liked me. She is my biggest fan. I have plenty of enemies, so to have a biggest fan is awesome. We all need *someone* in our corner. We have now been married over thirteen years, so that's a fantastic trend.

My children, Rachel and Max, crack me up. If my work inspires them to read and write more—as they love to do so far—then I will be very happy. If I can get them to make more deposits than withdrawals in the bank of life, I will have done my job as a parent. I am so proud of them.

My ghost writer, Dick Richards, helped me organize my investing thoughts as much as possible and spit out a great first draft of the book. Meghann Will helped with a ton of printing, organizing, and editing.

Finally, when your therapist starts picking stocks better than you, you take notice. When she could care less whether you are taking her ideas for your blog and book, you like her more. That "she" is Nancy Heinonen, my shrink and life coach. She did not sign up for the life stuff, just to clear a bunch of personal and relational stuff. She wanted to kick me out a thousand times, but I kept showing up with juicy problems. My life is good right now as I write, but no trend lasts forever, so I hedge once a week with my visits.

Hope you enjoy the book and that it helps you profit in many ways!

INDEX

venture capitalists (VCs), (*cont'd*)
   consumer robotics and, 178
   doing your homework and, 74–75
   health care and, 170–71
   human computer interface and,
     174–77
   information technology and, 160–62
   social leverage and, 188, 193–94
   trends and, 160–63
vice stocks, 143, 152–54
Viva.com!, 20

Wallstrip, how to use, 78–80
Wanger, Ralph, 61
war, wars, 10, 15
   trends and, 37, 143, 154–55
Waste Management, 101–2
WeightWatchers, 156

Wilcox, Cole:
   money management and, 93, 97
   trends and, 26
Wilson, Fred, 6, 74, 162–64, 189
   bear markets and, 113–14, 116, 118
   Internet and, 163–64
WorldCom, 14, 26, 29, 184
   money management and, 85–86
write-offs, 62

Yahoo!, 101, 167, 169, 174
   bear markets and, 115, 119
   doing your homework and, 73–74, 79
   social leverage and, 184
   trends and, 30, 41–42, 46, 55, 144–45
YouTube, 41, 46, 72, 169, 190

Zebra in Lion Country, A (Wanger), 61